Biological cycle

 Eggs laid singly

 Eggs laid in groups

 Caterpillar living in isolation

 Gregarious caterpillar

 Caterpillar feeding at night

 Chrysalis hidden within vegetal debris

 Chrysalis attached by its base, head upwards

 Chrysalis hanging head downwards

 Myrmecophilous caterpillar (living with ants)

 Non-myrmecophilous caterpillar

Timetable

| I |
| II |
| III | Month |
| IV |
| V |
| VI |
| VII |
| VIII |
| IX |
| X |
| XI |
| XII |

 Egg

 Caterpillar (larva)

 Chrysalis

Butterfly (imago)

 Caterpillar's foodplant

 Distribution

Butterflies
a colour field guide

M. Devarenne

English translation by Lucia Wildt

DAVID & CHARLES
Newton Abbot   London

CONTENTS

British Library Cataloguing in Publication Data

Devarenne, M.
Butterflies.
1. Butterflies—Europe—Identification
2. Insects—Europe—Identification
I. Title   II. Guide des papillons dans leurs
milieu   naturel. *English*
595.78'9'094   QL555.A1

ISBN o-7153-8488-0

Filmset by Keyspools Ltd, Golborne, Lancs
Printed in Belgium

INTRODUCTION

Since the dawn of time butterflies have been regarded as symbols of beauty and grace. Their marvellous colours and their harmonious shapes have inspired artists both ancient and modern—even the Egyptian frescoes showed remarkable numbers of butterflies. But it was only during the eighteenth century that the study of natural sciences took on a decisive impetus, particularly due to the contribution of the great Swedish naturalist Charles Linnaeus (1709–1778). He based the classification of animals and plants on the concepts of genus and species, and it is this classification which led to the reorganisation of huge collections of butterflies in museums throughout the world.

Today, we know of at least 140,000 species of butterfly, the majority being nocturnal ones (*Heterocera*) and the rest diurnal (*Rhopalocera*) which are often endowed with enchanting colours. While some butterflies are so common as to be regarded as a nuisance, others are extremely rare, occasionally almost extinct. In England, the drainage of the marshlands of Huntingdonshire and Cambridgeshire has contributed to the disappearance of the splendid *Lycaena dispar* (pl 32); miraculously, a very close subspecies was discovered in 1920 by a schoolmaster who was collecting insects in the marshes of Friesland, in Holland. This was probably the most exciting discovery of a European diurnal butterfly to have taken place this century. Today, the great 'fiery butterfly' (as the Dutch call it) survives in safety within its marvellous natural reserve: its habitat, impenetrable to man, provides it with perfect protection.

The study of butterflies is comparatively recent and now has an important ecological aspect. Thus a better knowledge of the first stages of the insect, ie of the egg, the caterpillar and the chrysalis, will allow future generations to admire these marvellous and fragile animals. The survival of rare species depends entirely on our goodwill. The twentieth century has been particularly damaging to nature: one does not have to be old-fashioned to recognise that our natural heritage has not been properly looked after. Motorways, tourism, the massive plantations of conifers and eucalyptus trees, the drainage of marshlands, the destruction of hedgerows, the woodland and scrubland fires which each year destroy thousands of acres, the chemical fertilisers and pesticides—all have contributed to the disappearance of several biotopes where, previously, flora and fauna had quietly evolved. Each natural habitat destroyed represents an incalculable loss for future generations. On the other hand, the biological role of butterflies is of paramount importance: the majority pollinate the flowers they feed on.

Butterfly collectors, therefore, would be well advised to lay down their nets, even though they can only affect the fauna in those places where a considerable concentration of insects can be found. This recently happened at Digne, in the Provençal Alps, where luckily both fauna and flora are now wholly protected. To collect great numbers of newly hatched females is tantamount to preventing them from laying eggs and therefore ensuring the survival of the species. Why not follow the example of the ornithologists and practise photography of rare species as an excellent alternative to such a damaging activity? Or why not contribute to the preservation of threatened species by trying to breed them?

A first important step is the protection, by law, of certain butterflies, but it must be associated with the preservation of the biotope in which the adult evolves and which provides the plants suitable to feed the caterpillars—worthwhile programme for tomorrow's entomologists. The courtship antics of the male of *Gonepteryx rhamni* (pl 14), which flies up high in the sky only to plunge suddenly into the grass where the female gets literally trampled; the airborne fighting of the males of *Charaxes jasius* (pl 39) defending their territory; the nuptial dance of the *Clossiana euphrosyne* (pl 57); the magnificent flight of so many butterflies; all these moving spectacles are nature's presents to us: let us show our gratitude by respecting and defending these threatened species.

This guide cannot be comprehensive; we had the difficult task of selecting over 300 species in Europe, part of Asia and northern Africa; those which are most frequently found in our woods, fields and mountains. The different species have been cleverly grouped together in the plates according to colour and shape.

The author would like to thank Dr J. Hutsebaut, H. de Wavrin, Josée Geudens, Pierre Rosman, Robert van de Merghel and Robert d'Hayer who greatly helped in the compilation of this guide.

Photograph credits: The photographs used for the cover and the majority of plates in this guide have been taken by the author; the others by:

Hellin de Wavrin 5 55 81 83 105 106 132 137
Robert van de Merghel 22 32 33 80 89 111 112
Dr J. Hutsebaut 25

Cover illustration: Purple Emperor (*Apatura iris*)/(*M. Devarenne*)

HOW TO USE THIS GUIDE

The whole concept behind this guide is to offer a useful tool to ramblers and nature lovers who would like to know more about the marvellous world of diurnal butterflies. The pictograms accompanying each plate enable the reader to discover at a glance all the interesting facts relating to the biology and the behaviour of that particular butterfly and, most importantly, each colour photograph shows the insect *alive* within its natural habitat. For ease of reference, the colours indicated at the edge of the page depict the main ground colour of the insect's wings.

Any naturalist wishing to explore the varied and glittering world of butterflies must above all possess a keen sense of observation and a lot of patience. Some of them are quite shy and should be approached quietly and gently. Others are more friendly and fond of well-stocked gardens where they feed, for instance, on the flowers of buddleias (*Buddleia davidii*).

HOW TO READ THE SYMBOLS

Frequency or rarity of the species

Habitat and customs   Biological cycle   Timetable of the life cycle

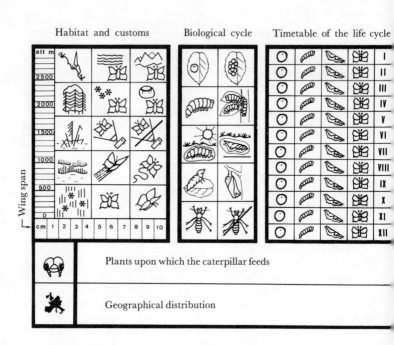

| | Plants upon which the caterpillar feeds |
| | Geographical distribution |

Frequency or rarity of the species

Butterfly protected by law

Rare or localised butterfly

Widely spread and quite common

Habitat

 Grassy banks, ravines, rocky paths in mountainous regions

 Wooded areas where various herbs and aromatic plants grow

 Damp and boggy fields, marshes, lagoons

 Heaths and tundras

 Wild open fields with plenty of flowers

 Butterfly living in coastal areas

 Butterfly indigenous to mountainous areas

 Altitudes at which butterflies and their foodplants can be found (in m)

Average span of fore-wings from tip to tip (in cm)

cm	1	2	3	4	5	6	7	8	9	10

Habits and behaviour

 Feeding on flower nectar

 Feeding on ripe fruits and certain refuse

 Friendly species

7

Very shy species

 Butterfly with rapid and determined flight

 Butterfly with slow and heavy flight

 Sedentary butterfly

 Migratory butterfly

Biological cycle—first stages

 Eggs laid singly

 Eggs laid in groups often of over one hundred

 Caterpillar living in isolation

 Caterpillars living in groups near a nest within which they take refuge at the first sign of danger. This communal life comes to an end when the larvae reach adulthood.

 Caterpillars feeding mainly at sunset and dawn or in wet or overcast weather.

 Chrysalis hidden within vegetal debris. The hatched butterfly will have to burrow a passage and find a support upon which to spread its wings.

 Chrysalis attached by its base and thorax, the head upwards.

 Chrysalis hanging head downwards by its cremaster, a kind of small abdominal hook attached to a tiny pad of silk.

Myrmecophilous caterpillars spending their cycle inside an anthill; as a reward for the sugary droplets they secrete, which are much appreciated by the ants, they feed on the eggs. Sometimes the ants follow the caterpillars on to the plant and defend them; thanks to this symbiosis, the caterpillars are protected from certain parasites always on the look-out.

Non-myrmecophilous caterpillars

Timetable (month)

1. The egg

2. The caterpillar or larva

3. The chrysalis

4. The adult butterfly (imago)

Foodplants

Plants upon which the larvae feed until they turn to chrysalides.

Geographical distribution

Distribution of the species within Europe, the Mediterranean islands, Africa, Asia, America and Canada.

BRIEF INTRODUCTION TO THE STUDY OF BUTTERFLIES

THE INITIAL STAGES OF DIURNAL BUTTERFLIES

The life-span of the adult insect, or *imago*, is relatively short when compared with its initial stages which manifest themselves under three guises:

1. The egg

As soon as the male has fertilised the female, the latter immediately looks for the host plant which will feed the caterpillars. The eggs are laid either in small groups or singly, according to the habits of the caterpillar. The magnifying glass discloses a large variety of shapes and colours and certain eggs appear to be real works of art. The eggs hatch rapidly, sometimes within a few days: the colour of the egg darkens and the small caterpillar appears.

2. The caterpillar

This is the most important and the most vulnerable stage in the life of the butterfly. Right from the beginning the caterpillar is threatened by innumerable predators: a certain amount of protection is afforded by its mimetic qualities, but by no means enough. Some caterpillars build nests within which to shelter at the first sign of danger; others secrete toxic substances which they extract from the plant they feed on. Thus they feel protected from birds, reptiles or small mammals which are constantly looking for them. In the case of certain species, the ecological balance is maintained by the presence of predatory insects belonging to the Hymenoptera order (genus Ichneumon), as well as some dipterous ones. The former lay their eggs within or on the caterpillars, which, nonetheless, continue to grow, albeit more slowly. Eventually the caterpillar, sometimes covered in small cocoons, dies on its host plant; in some cases, it does turn into a chrysalis, but it is the parasite that will finally emerge. Each caterpillar is provided with some form of protection; sometimes this is in the shape of an organ called an osmeterium which is situated on the back of the head and emits a strong smell to scare off potential predators. In other cases the caterpillars possess hairs which can sting and burn. Some of the caterpillars of the Lycaenidae are protected by the ants with which they live in symbiosis. The destructive species (and there are some) seem to suffer from epidemics which kill them off in huge numbers:

they can then be seen hanging lifeless from the trees. This is the case, for instance, of nocturnal butterflies belonging to the genus Bombicyna (the processional moth of the pine trees) and the genus Lymantriidae (the destroyer of holm oaks in the Mediterranean regions).

Diurnal butterflies do not produce such destructive caterpillars; however, the larvae of the Large White (pl 20), the Black-veined White (pl 19) and the Large Tortoiseshell (pl 40) can become a nuisance through their sheer numbers in favourable years. It is the larvae which are affected by the tons of pesticides and insecticides which are scattered over the countryside. In some European areas, the decrease in the butterfly population is quite frightening. This is particularly so in northern Greece where excellent biotopes are seriously threatened by agriculture.

The majority of caterpillars feed at sunset or dawn; during the day they remain attached to a pad of silk previously woven. During their cycle they are subject to various moultings (sometimes five or six), their patterns and colour changing at each one. Just before turning into a chrysalis, in its pre-nymphatic stage, the caterpillar attaches itself to a support, turns a strange colour and loses its skin.

3. The chrysalis

The chrysalis is either attached, head upwards, by a silky belt; hangs, head downwards, by its small hooks (cremaster) from a previously woven silky pad; or hides amongst vegetal debris. The chrysalides of diurnal butterflies are not protected by a cocoon, like those of the nocturnal ones; the chrysalis of the Apollo (pl 8) can usually be found in the soil within a cavity lined with a few strands of silk, but not in a proper cocoon. Undoubtedly, the only protection is mimetism: sometimes the chrysalides of the same species assume different colours according to the support chosen by the caterpillar. Shortly before the emergence of the butterfly, the latter's colours can be detected through the chrysalis.

The butterfly then spreads its fragile wings, the nervatures fill with liquid, and a few drops of meconium are shed. Once the wings are dry, the insect launches itself on its maiden flight.

THE VARIOUS FAMILIES
1. The Papilionidae

The swallowtail butterflies are extremely beautiful: *Papilio machaon* (pl 1) and *Iphiclides podalirius* (pl 4) flutter on the flowers of fallow fields. Other representatives of this sumptuous family are *Parnassius apollo* (pl 8) which lives in the mountains, *Zerynthia polyxena* (pl 6) and *Z. ruminia* (pl 7) which can be found on damp meadows and moors. Their eggs look like tiny soft-coloured pearls; they are laid in isolation or, very occasionally in small groups. The often highly coloured caterpillars sit motionless on thin stems. They are mercilessly hunted by a parasitic insect belonging to the Hymenoptera order, the ichneumon, which lays its eggs in the caterpillar's body. The ichneumon's larva develops inside the caterpillar and subsequently inside the chrysalis, from which it will emerge. The only defence the caterpillar has is an organ called osmeterium situated on its back: it is only noticeable at the slightest cause of alarm, when it emits a particular smell designed to ward off predators. The chrysalides are quite substantial; they are perfectly mimetised with the support from which they hang, head upwards, by means of a fragile silk loop. The chrysalis of *Parnassius apollo* is usually found in the soil.

2. The Pieridae

These lepidoptera, commonly called 'The Whites', are well known and often confused with one another. With the first fine weather the Brimstone (pl 14) brightens the woodlands which are just beginning to wake from winter slumber. In gardens *Pieris rapae* (pl 21) *P. napi* (pl 22) announce the oncoming of spring with their presence. Some pierids are great migrators. At the beginning of this century, in England, a large swarm of migrating *Pieris brassicae* (pl 20) managed to interrupt a game of cricket. In Europe, pierids gather on humid soils in groups which rarely exceed one hundred individuals, but I remember having seen them in Amazonia thickly gathered on a bank over an area of almost one hundred metres. *Colias palaeno* (pl 11) has vanished from several habitats where it was once common and is now a rare species. Its eggs are elongated and of a soft colour which perfectly mimetises them within their environment. The caterpillars of the pierids are smooth and often live in colonies. The chrysalides often fasten themselves to tree-trunks and walls.

3. The Danaidae

This interesting family comprises some 300 species, mainly living in tropical regions. Two species can be found in Europe and northern Africa in the desert areas: the *Danaus plexippus*, a great migrator but which rarely reaches continental Europe (it is well adapted to the Canary Islands), and *Danaus chrysippus* (pl 37) which is widely spread over the arid regions of northern Africa. A peculiar characteristic of the danaids is the toxic substances with which caterpillars, chrysalides and adult insects are endowed. These substances originate from the foodplants of the splendid caterpillar which, despite its striking appearance, is perfectly protected from birds, reptiles and small mammals. This kind of protection is present in the chrysalis, which looks like a precious stone, and in the adult butterfly fluttering on the swallow-worts on which it feeds. In certain tropical regions, the females of other genera resemble the danaids in colour and wing-design and find themselves thus protected against predators. This extraordinary phenomenon is called batesian mimicry. The male has a black scale, the androconial gland, on the hind-wing. When mating, the male literally lifts the female up in flight.

4. The Libytheidae

The only representative of this small, mainly South American, family to be found in southern Europe is *Libythea celtis* (pl 38). It is very common in Greece and Turkey. The butterfly, having spent the winter in a sheltered place such as a barn, a sheepfold or the hollow of an old tree-trunk, flies off quickly during the first fine days. The females look for nettle-trees (*Celtis australis*) on which the eggs are laid in small groups. The tiny caterpillars build a silky nest in which they hide at the first sign of danger or to protect them from torrential rain. The darkly coloured caterpillars are gregarious and almost entirely devour their host plant. Cuckoos and related birds are very fond of these caterpillars, whose metamorphosis takes place on the larger branches or on the trunk of the nettle-tree. The chrysalides are perfectly mimetic thanks to their colour which merges with their support; they hang briefly by means of their cremaster.

5. The Nymphalidae

This is one of the largest groups, represented on all continents; in Europe it includes various showy species, including the splendid, fiery Red Admirals and the Purple Emperors with their beautiful blue reflections on the brown background of their wings. Unlike their cousins the *Nymphalidae* do not move about on their six legs. In fact, in the majority of cases the two fore-legs have no apparent function in either sex. The caterpillars often spend the first stages of their mutation in groups within a silky nest in which they find refuge from the weather and from danger. While some of them overwinter as caterpillars the Red Admirals spend the winter as adult insects within cavities, barns, haylofts, and similar buildings. On the other hand, the Purple Emperors (pls 90 and 91) and the Poplar and White Admirals (pls 87, 88 and 89) hibernate as tiny brown caterpillars hidden in a rolled-up leaf.

Some of the caterpillars have thorns on their backs; others are smooth. There are also several varieties of chrysalides: those of the Red Admirals are angular, those of the Purple Emperors resemble a rolled leaf. They are usually suspended at the base, anchored by their cremaster.

6. The Satyridae

The European representatives of this family are neither particularly noticeable for their bright colours nor for the interesting shape of their wings. On the contrary, their rather dull colour would hardly attract any attention. On closer inspection, however, it is possible to observe on their wings certain round spots which do much to enhance their discreet beauty. Some of these species are very localised, for example the Arran Brown (pl 104) or the rare Scarce Heath (pl 108). On the other hand, some are so common on fallow lands and flowery meadows that the slightest movement will send a whole cloud of them into the air. Examples are the Meadow Brown (pl 72) and the Small

Heath (pl 74). The eggs are usually laid on grasses (Graminaceae): they are finely ribbed and pale in colour. The fusiform caterpillar has a double-pointed abdomen and its green or brownish colour serves as an excellent camouflage. The chrysalis can usually be found among vegetal debris; sometimes, but rarely, it is suspended by the cremaster from a silky pad previously woven by the caterpillar during its pre-pupal stage.

7. The Nemeobiidae

There are about 2,000 species of this family, mainly living in the tropical regions of South America. Only one species, the Duke of Burgundy Fritillary (pl 80), belongs to the European fauna; softly coloured, its brownish hue causes it to be confused with the butterflies of the genus *Melitae* with which it often shares its habitat. The eggs are deposited in small groups on the leaves of primulas; shortly before they hatch their colour becomes slightly darker and fine lines appear on the surface. The brownish caterpillar spends the day at the foot of the host plant, avoiding the sun's rays and feeding at dawn or twilight. The chrysalis is off-white with black spots and fine hairs on the back. At this stage this Fritillary hibernates among vegetal debris in the soil.

8. The Lycaenidae

A walk through fields and woods will reveal these butterflies belonging to the groups of the Blues and the Coppers. Their small glittering wings help brighten up the countryside. In clearings and woodland borders, another genus, the Hairstreak, flutters here and there among the shrubs and brambles. This family also includes the Green Hairstreak (pl 124), a rare butterfly with a green underside, which, once it has settled on foliage, is impossible to distinguish from its surroundings.

The larval stage of this family is particularly interesting. In 1916, after many efforts to breed the Alcon Blue (pl 130) and the beautiful Large Blue (pl 131), the naturalists Powell and Chapman discovered the solution to what had been a real enigma through their patient observations carried out on site. Having noticed a strange coming and going of ants all round the host plants, they tried to breed the caterpillars in captivity by feeding them on ant larvae and eggs. Thus part of the mystery was solved, but still the strange phenomenon had to be understood. Subsequent detailed studies have led to a greater understanding of this case. The caterpillars possess a honey gland which exudes droplets of sweet liquid much sought after by the ants; they stimulate the gland by massaging it with their antennae and their legs. In return the ants provide the caterpillars with the eggs and larvae on which they feed. Depending on the various species, the caterpillars are either taken into the ants' nest or are visited on their own host plants. The ants further protect the caterpillars against their indefatigable predators, the ichneumons—hymenopterous insects which lay their eggs inside or on the caterpillars.

However, not all the *Lycaenidae* have to live in ants' nests in order to reach their larval maturity, but the absence of ants can alter to a certain extent the development of some of them. On the other hand, the cycle of the Large Copper (pl 32) can develop quite independently. The chrysalis is small and can be found sometimes in the soil or in the upper galleries of the ants' nest, or, more often, on the foodplant to which it is attached by a fine silky loop.

9. The Hesperiidae

Because of their structure, this family has been classified as the most primitive in evolution. *Hesperiidae* occur in all geographical regions of the world; some species are so primitive that the male possesses the structures of a nocturnal butterfly (*Heterocera*) while the female has the characteristics of a diurnal one. The swelling on their antennae is characteristic of nocturnal butterflies but their habits are essentially diurnal. The *Hesperiidae* can easily be distinguished from related species by their extremely rapid and sometimes skipping flight, which makes them difficult to see. They can be admired when they settle to feed on thistles and brambles.

The Large Chequered Skipper (pl 122) is one of the most localised species in this guide. The eggs, spherical with a flattened base, are mainly laid on Graminaceae and Malvaceae; here the caterpillar develops, an elongated creature with a blackish or brownish head which builds itself a nest as a refuge against the weather. The smooth chrysalides are mainly to be found in the soil, among vegetal debris, or on a stem surrounded by a few leaves tied together with a silky thread.

PLATES

The information in the pictograms underneath each plate is supplemented by an appendix (p 161) which provides brief details on the ecology, sexual dimorphism and variants of each species.

Abbreviations: ♂ = male
♀ = female

Papilio machaon L. ♂   Papilionidae

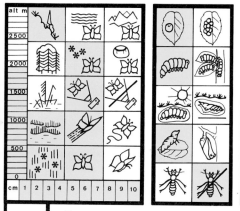

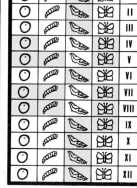

 Common carrot (*Daucus carota*), fennel (*Foeniculum vulgare*), parsleys (*Peucedanums*), angelicas and rues.

 Northern Africa, Europe, Asia as far as Japan.

Papilio hospiton Géné ♂   Papilionidae

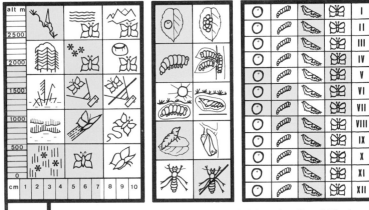

Wild Umbelliferae, especially, at certain heights, giant fennel (*Ferula communis*) and Corsican rue (*Ruta corsica*).

Endemic to Corsica and Sardinia.

Papilio alexanor Esper ♂   Papilionidae

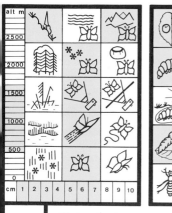

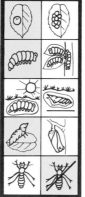

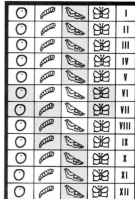

 Various Umbelliferae, including seselis (*Seseli montanum*), *Ptychotis heterophylla* and *Trinia vulgaris*.

 South-east of France, southern Italy, Sicily, south of the Balkans from Iran to Turkestan.

Iphiclides podalirius L. ♀   Papilionidae

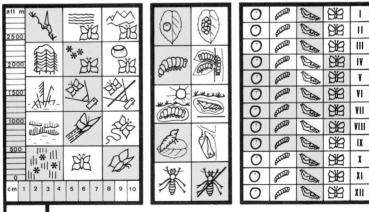

 Sloe tree (*Prunus spinosa*), hawthorn (*Crataegus oxyacantha*) and various fruit trees.

Central and southern Europe as far as Asia.

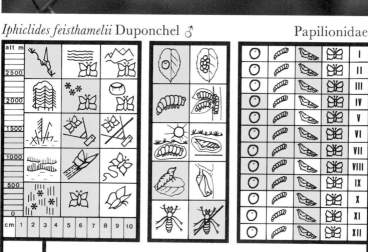

Iphiclides feisthamelii Duponchel ♂

Papilionidae

Hawthorn (*Crataegus oxyacantha*) and other Rosaceae. Fruit trees.

Northern Africa, Iberian Peninsula. The two species, *I. podalirius* and *I. feisthamelii*, rarely share the same habitat.

Zerynthia polyxena Schiffermüller ♀   Papilionidae

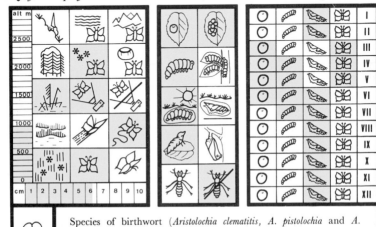

Species of birthwort (*Aristolochia clematitis, A. pistolochia* and *A. rotunda*).

From central and southern Europe to Asia Minor.

Zerynthia rumina L. ♂　　　　　　　　　　Papilionidae

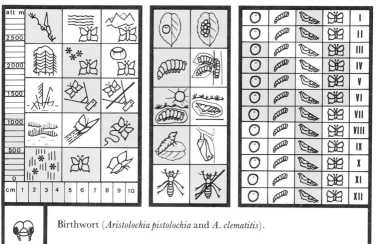

Birthwort (*Aristolochia pistolochia* and *A. clematitis*).

Northern Africa, south-west Europe.

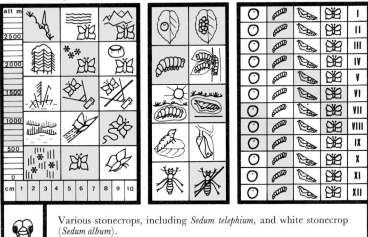

Parnassius apollo L. ♂   Papilionidae

Various stonecrops, including *Sedum telephium*, and white stonecrop (*Sedum album*).

Mountainous regions from Europe to Central Asia.

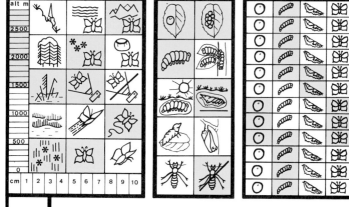

Parnassius phoebus Stichel ♂

Papilionidae

 Sempervivum montanum and various saxifrages (*Saxifraga*).

Alps, Urals, Siberia, Kamchatka; North America in the Rocky Mountains.

Anthocharis belia L. ssp. *euphenoides* Staudinger ♂   Pieridae

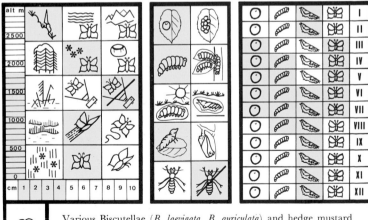

 Various Biscutellae (*B. laevigata*, *B. auriculata*) and hedge mustard (*Sisymbrium*).

Northern Africa (*A. belia belia* L.); southern Europe (*A. euphenoides* Staudinger).

Colias palaeno L. ♀   Pieridae

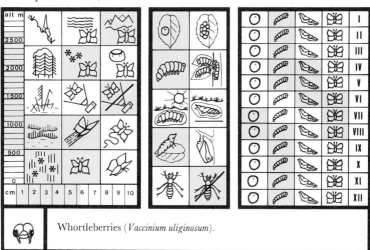

	Whortleberries (*Vaccinium uliginosum*).
🦋	From central and northern Europe to Siberia.

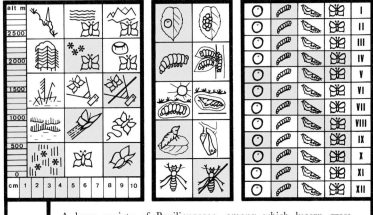

Colias hyale L. ♂   Pieridae

 A large variety of Papilionaceae, among which lucern grass (*Medicago*) and clovers (*Trifolium*) as well as vetches (*Vicia*).

From western Europe to Russia as far as the Altai mountains.

Colias australis Verity ♂   Pieridae

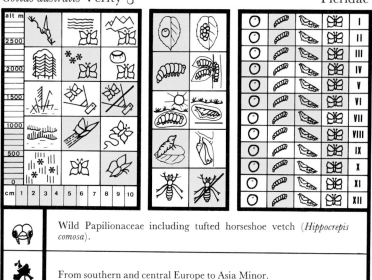

Wild Papilionaceae including tufted horseshoe vetch (*Hippocrepis comosa*).

From southern and central Europe to Asia Minor.

Gonepteryx rhamni L. ♂   Pieridae

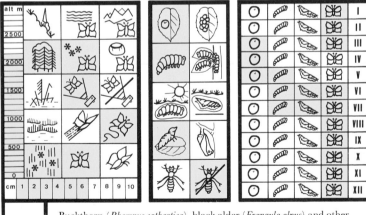

 Buckthorn (*Rhamnus cathartica*), black alder (*Frangula alnus*) and other Rhamnaceae.

 From northern Africa to western Europe; Russia, Siberia and Asia Minor.

Gonepteryx cleopatra L. ssp. *europaea* Verity ♂ Pieridae

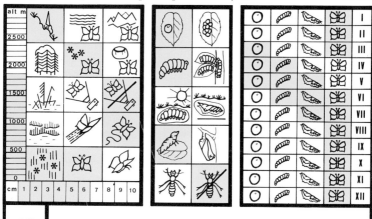

 Buckthorn (*Rhamnus cathartica*) and other Rhamnaceae.

 Northern Africa, Madeira and the Canary Islands (*G. cleopatra cleopatra* L.); southern Europe as far as Asia Minor (*G. cleopatra* ssp. *europaea* Verity).

Melanargia galathea L. ♂   Satyridae

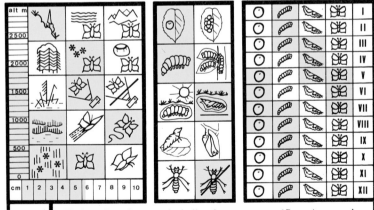

 Various Graminaceae, including brome grasses (*Bromus*), annual meadow grasses (*Poa annua*), sheep's fescue (*Festuca ovina*) and orchard grass (*Dactylis glomerata*).

 From western Europe to southern Russia and northern Iran.

Melanargia occitanica Esper ♂   Satyridae

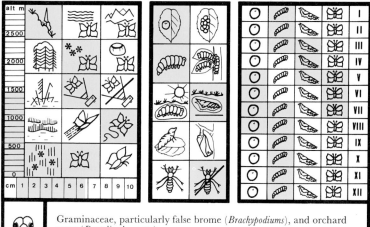

 Graminaceae, particularly false brome (*Brachypodiums*), and orchard grass (*Dactylis glomerata*).

South-west Europe, North Africa.

Parnassius mnemosyne L. ♂   Papilionidae

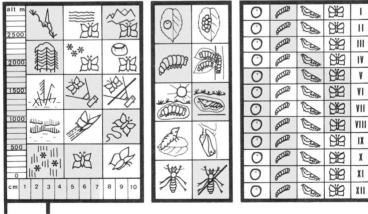

 Corydalis and various plants belonging to the Papaveraceae.

Spanish Pyrenees, central France, northern Europe; Asia Minor, Iran, Caucasus.

Aporia crataegi L. ♂   Pieridae

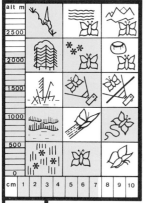

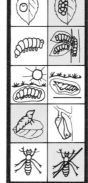

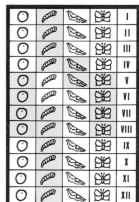

 Hawthorn (*Crataegus oxyacantha*), may (*Crataegus monogyna*), very occasionally on sloe (*Prunus spinosa*) and fruit trees.

 Northern Africa (Morocco and Algeria), western Europe, Korea and Japan.

Pieris brassicae L. ♂   Pieridae

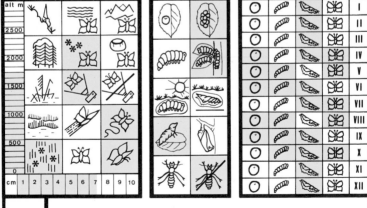

Resedaceae and a large number of Cruciferae. The caterpillar can cause serious damage on a large scale.

From northern Africa to Europe and Asia as far as the Himalayas.

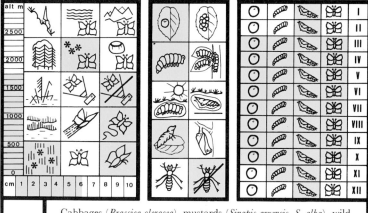

Pieris rapae L. ♂   Pieridae

Cabbages (*Brassica oleracea*), mustards (*Sinapis arvensis, S. alba*), wild radishes (*Raphanus raphanstrum*) and other Cruciferae and Resedaceae.

Northern Africa, Europe, and as far as Asia and Japan; introduced in North America.

Pieris napi L. ♂　　　　　　　　　　Pieridae

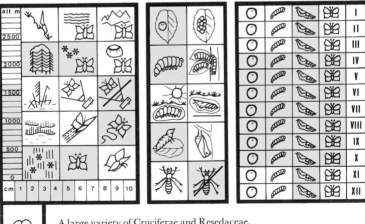

　A large variety of Cruciferae and Resedaceae.

Northern Africa, Europe, Asia as far as Japan, North America.

Pontia daplidice L. ♂   Pieridae

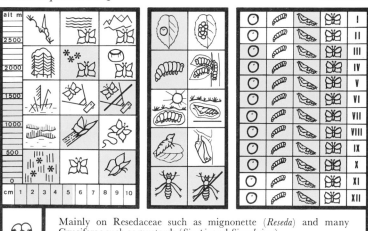

 Mainly on Resedaceae such as mignonette (*Reseda*) and many Cruciferae such as mustards (*Sinapis* and *Sisymbrium*).

 From Africa to southern Europe and as far as India and Japan.

Colotis evagore nouna Lucas ♀   Pieridae

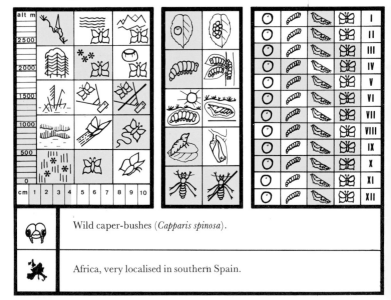

Wild caper-bushes (*Capparis spinosa*).

Africa, very localised in southern Spain.

Anthocharis cardamines L. ♂   Pieridae

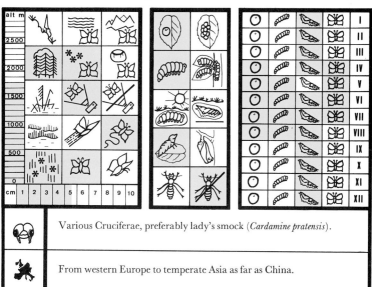

Various Cruciferae, preferably lady's smock (*Cardamine pratensis*).

From western Europe to temperate Asia as far as China.

Euchloe ausonia Hübner ♂   Pieridae

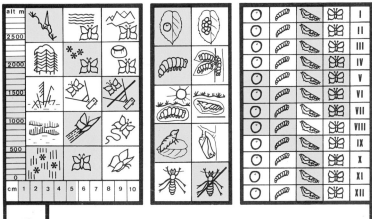

 Many Cruciferae, above all the genus *Iberis* (candytuft).

North Africa, from Europe to R. Amur, North America, Alaska, Colorado, Arizona.

Euchloe belemia Esper ♂ Pieridae

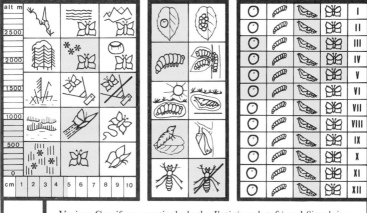

 Various Cruciferae, particularly the *Iberis* (candytuft) and *Sisymbrium* (hedge mustard) genera.

 South-west Europe, northern Africa, Tibesti mtns, Iran and Baluchistan.

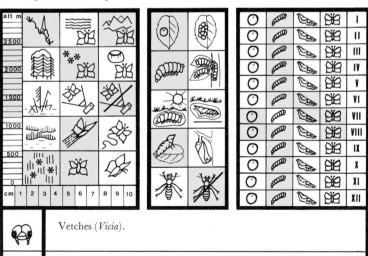

Colias phicomone Esper ♂   Pieridae

Vetches (*Vicia*).

Europe.

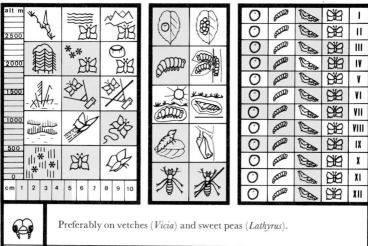

Leptidea sinapis L. ♂   Pieridae

 Preferably on vetches (*Vicia*) and sweet peas (*Lathyrus*).

 Morocco, western Europe as far as the Caucasus and Syria.

Colias crocea Fourcroy ♀   Pieridae

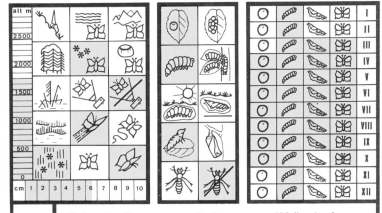

Various Papilionaceae, namely lucern grass (*Medicago*), clovers (*Trifolium*), melilots (*Melilotus*), bird's-foot trefoil (*Lotus*).

Northern Africa, Fezzan, Cyrenaica; southern and central Europe towards the east as far as western Asia and Iran.

Lycaena phlaeas L. ♂   Lycaenidae

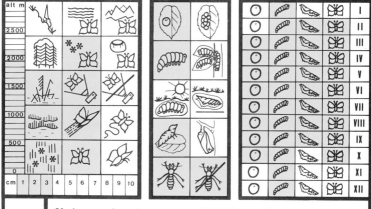

 Various sorrels, such as wood sorrel (*Oxalis acetosella*), common sorrel (*Rumex acetosa*), and docks (*Rumex crispus, R. acetosella, R. obtusifolius*).

 From North Africa to Kenya; from Europe to temperate Asia and Japan; North America.

Lycaena dispar Haworth ssp. *batava* Oberthur ♂
ssp. *rutila* Wernerberg   Lycaenidae

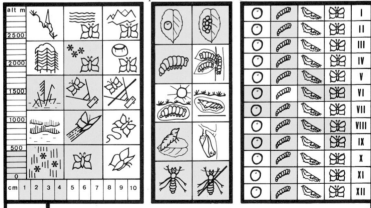

 Various docks and sorrels (*Rumex crispus, R. hydrolapathum, R. aquaticus*), plants growing by the side of streams and in bogs. Also *Rumex sanguineus*.

 From western Europe to Russia as far as R. Amur.

Heodes virgaureae L. ♂   Lycaenidae

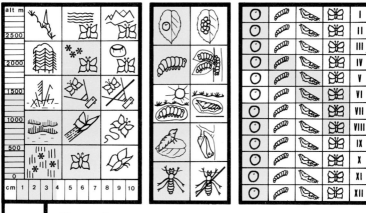

Various wild sorrels and docks (*Rumex acetosa, R. acetosella*) and certain Polygonaceae.

From Europe and Asia Minor to central Asia as far as Mongolia.

Heodes alciphron Rottemburg ♂   Lycaenidae

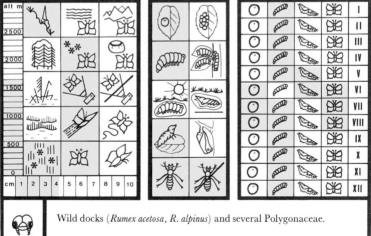

 Wild docks (*Rumex acetosa*, *R. alpinus*) and several Polygonaceae.

From western Europe to Asia Minor as far as Iran.

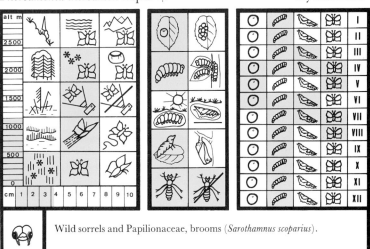

Thersamonia thersamon Esper ♀   Lycaenidae

 Wild sorrels and Papilionaceae, brooms (*Sarothamnus scoparius*).

From Italy and eastern Europe to Iraq and Iran.

Paleochrysophanus hippothoe L. ♀   Lycaenidae

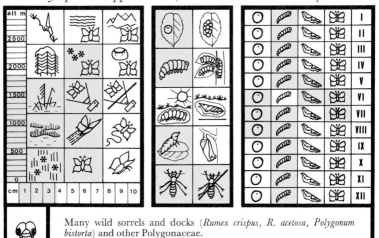

Many wild sorrels and docks (*Rumex crispus, R. acetosa, Polygonum bistorta*) and other Polygonaceae.

From Europe to Siberia and R. Amur.

Danaus chrysippus L. ♂   Danaidae

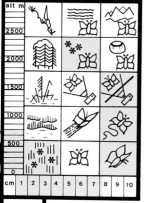

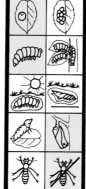

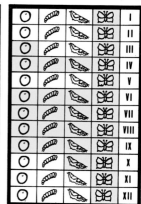

 The swallow-wort (*Asclepia*), a poisonous plant which ensures the safety of the caterpillars.

 Africa, Arabia and as far as tropical Asia and Australia. Can be seen in the Canary Islands.

Libythea celtis Laicharting ♂   Libytheidae

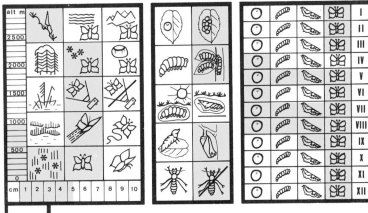

	The nettle-tree (*Celtis australis*) and cherry tree (*Prunus cerasus*).	
	Southern Europe, northern Africa to Asia Minor, Siberia, Formosa and Japan.	

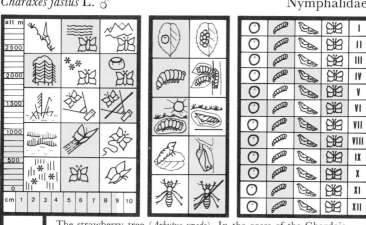

Charaxes jasius L. ♂   Nymphalidae

The strawberry tree (*Arbutus unedo*). In the oases of the Ghardaia region in Algeria, the caterpillars have adapted to the leaves of orange trees.

Mediterranean regions as far as Ethiopia and equatorial Africa where various subspecies can be found.

Nymphalis polychloros L. ♂   Nymphalidae

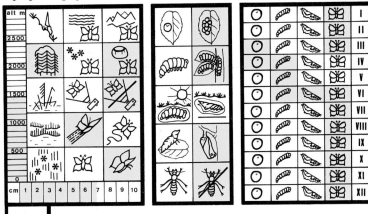

Elms (*Ulmus*), willows (*Salix*) and fruiting trees.

Northern Africa, central and southern Europe, from Asia Minor to the Himalayas.

Inachis io L. ♀   Nymphalidae

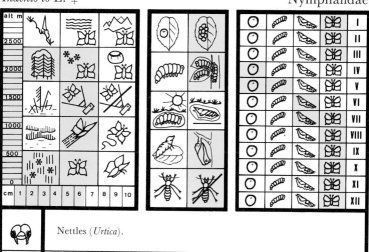

Nettles (*Urtica*).

From Europe to temperate Asia and as far as Japan.

Aglais urticae L. ♂   Nymphalidae

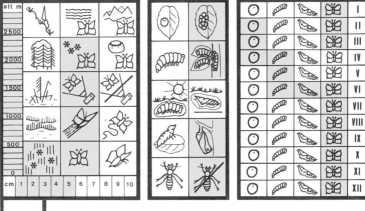

Nettles (*Urtica*), elms (*Ulmus*), willows (*Salix*) and some fruiting trees.

From western Europe to the Pacific coast of Asia.

Vanessa cardui L. ♂　　　　　　　　　　　Nymphalidae

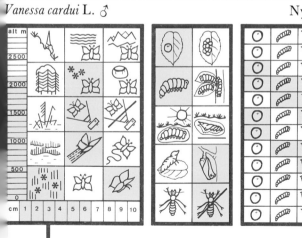

 Thistles (*Cardus*), nettles (*Urtica*) and mallows (*Malva*).

 All over the world except for South America.

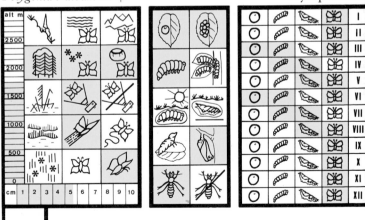

Polygonia c-album L. ♀   Nymphalidae

Nettles (*Urtica*) and elms (*Ulmus*).

Northern Africa, Europe; as far as China and Japan.

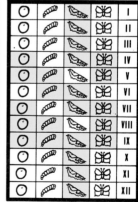

Araschnia levana L. ♂   Nymphalidae

○	🐛	🦋	🦋	I
○	🐛	🦋	🦋	II
○	🐛	🦋	🦋	III
○	🐛	🦋	🦋	IV
○	🐛	🦋	🦋	V
○	🐛	🦋	🦋	VI
○	🐛	🦋	🦋	VII
○	🐛	🦋	🦋	VIII
○	🐛	🦋	🦋	IX
○	🐛	🦋	🦋	X
○	🐛	🦋	🦋	XI
○	🐛	🦋	🦋	XII

Nettles (*Urtica*).

From Europe eastwards through Asia as far as Japan.

Pandoriana pandora Schiffermüller ♂   Nymphalidae

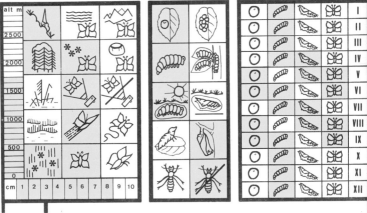

 Pansies (*Viola*), particularly heartsease (*Viola tricolor*).

 Canary Islands, northern Africa, southern Europe, southern Russia, Iran, Tian-Chan.

Argynnis paphia L. ♂ Nymphalidae

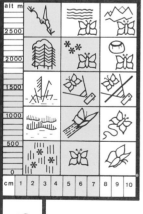

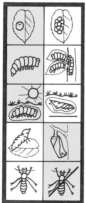

Pansies and violets (*Viola*).

Western Europe, Algeria, temperate Asia, Japan.

Mesoacidalia aglaja L. ♂   Nymphalidae

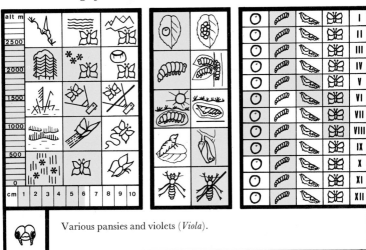

Various pansies and violets (*Viola*).

From Morocco and western Europe to China and Japan.

Fabriciana adippe Schiffermüller ♂   Nymphalidae

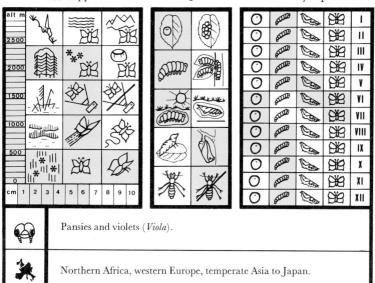

Pansies and violets (*Viola*).

Northern Africa, western Europe, temperate Asia to Japan.

Fabriciana niobe L. ♂   Nymphalidae

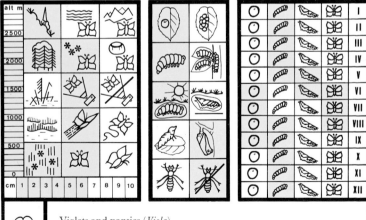

 Violets and pansies (*Viola*).

Algeria and Morocco, western Europe, Russia to Asia Minor and Iran.

Fabriciana elisa Godart ♂   Nymphalidae

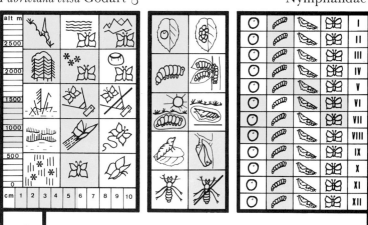

 Various violets (*Viola*).

 Endemic to Corsica and Sardinia.

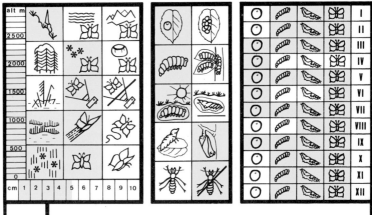

Issoria lathonia L. ♂   Nymphalidae

 Violets (*Viola*), borage (*Borago officinalis*) and nettles (*Urtica*).

 Canary Islands, northern Africa, western Europe, Asia to the Himalayas and western China.

Brenthis daphne Schiffermüller ♂ .... Nymphalidae

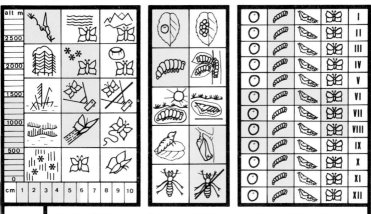

 Violets (*Viola*), as well as certain Rosaceae such as wild raspberry (*Rubus idaeus*) and blackberry (*Rubus*).

 Southern and eastern Europe as far as Asia.

Boloria pales **Schiffermüller** ♂   Nymphalidae

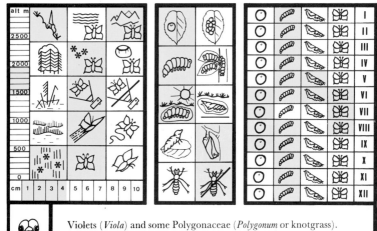

Violets (*Viola*) and some Polygonaceae (*Polygonum* or knotgrass).

Cantabrian mountains, Pyrenees, Alps, Carpathians, Caucasus, Central Asia to China.

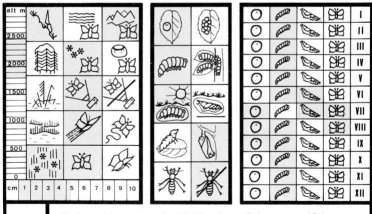

Boloria napaea Hoffmansegg ♂   Nymphalidae

 Various violets and pansies (*Viola*) and some Polygonaceae (*Polygonum* or knotgrass).

 Eastern Pyrenees, Alps, Scandinavia as far as the North Cape; eastwards to the Altai mountains and R. Amur; North America from Alaska to Wyoming.

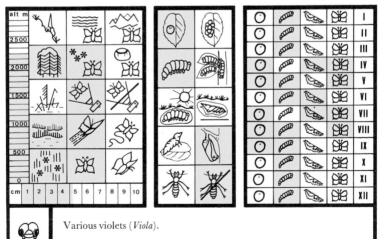

Clossiana selene Schiffermüller ♂   Nymphalidae

Various violets (*Viola*).

From western Europe through Asia as far as Korea; North America.

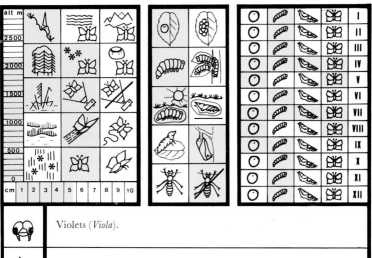

Clossiana euphrosyne L. ♂   Nymphalidae

Violets (*Viola*).

Western Europe to R. Amur and the Kamchatka.

Brenthis ino **Rottemburg** ♀   Nymphalidae

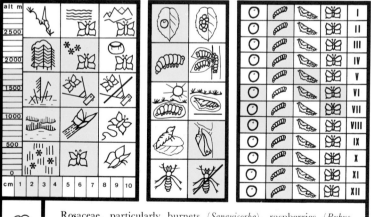

Rosaceae, particularly burnets (*Sanguisorba*), raspberries (*Rubus idaeus*), meadowsweet (*Filipendula ulmaria*), and nettles (*Urtica*).

Throughout Europe as far as Asia.

Clossiana dia L. ♀　　　　　　　　　　Nymphalidae

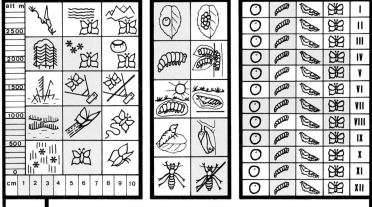

 Various violets (*Viola*), raspberries (*Rubus idaeus*), self-heal (*Prunella vulgaris*) and several Labiatae.

 From Morocco and western Europe to China.

Melitaea cinxia L. ♂   Nymphalidae

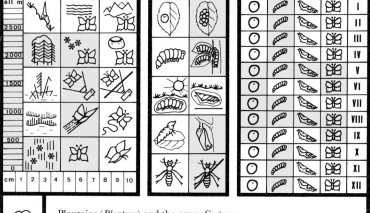

 Plantains (*Plantago*) and the genus *Centaurea*.

 Morocco, from western Europe to Russia as far as R. Amur.

Melitaea phoebe Schiffermüller ♂   Nymphalidae

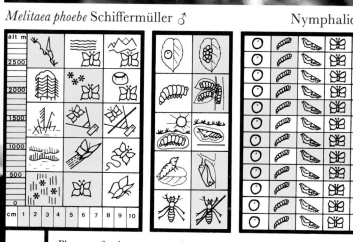

Plants of the genera *Centaurea* (knapweed) and *Plantago* (plantains).

Northern Africa, Europe, central Asia, northern China.

Melitaea didyma Esper ♀   Nymphalidae

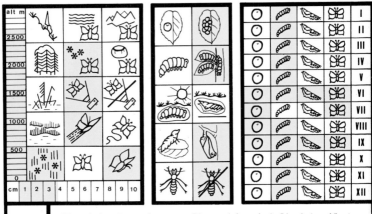

Plants belonging to the genera *Plantago* (plantains), *Linaria* (toadflax) and *Veronica* (speedwell).

Northern Africa as far as Tripolitania, Fezzan and Tibesti. Europe, mainly in the south, Russia and Turkestan.

Melitaea diamina Lang ♂   Nymphalidae

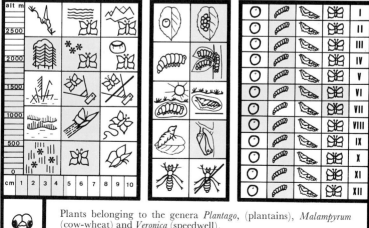

 Plants belonging to the genera *Plantago*, (plantains), *Malampyrum* (cow-wheat) and *Veronica* (speedwell).

From western Europe to Asia.

Mellicta athalia Rottemburg ♀   Nymphalidae

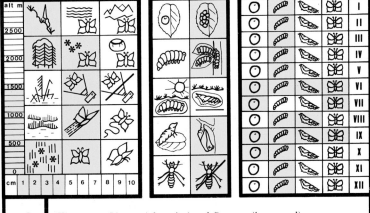

 The genera *Plantago* (plantains) and *Centaurea* (knapweed).

From western Europe to Russia and temperate areas of Asia as far as Japan.

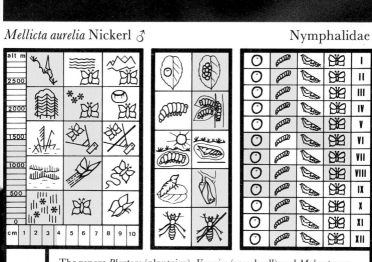

Mellicta aurelia Nickerl ♂   Nymphalidae

 The genera *Plantago* (plantains), *Veronica* (speedwell) and *Malampyrum* (cow-wheat).

 Mainly central Europe as far as the Urals, Caucasus and central Asia.

Euphydryas maturna L. ♂   Nymphalidae

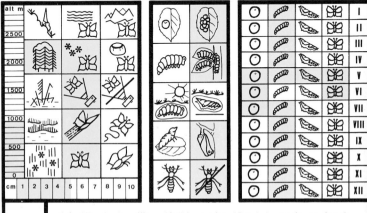

 Ash (*Fraxinus*), willow (*Salix*), poplar (*Populus*), rarely on beech (*Fagus*).

From Europe to Russia as far as the Ala Tau and Altai mountains.

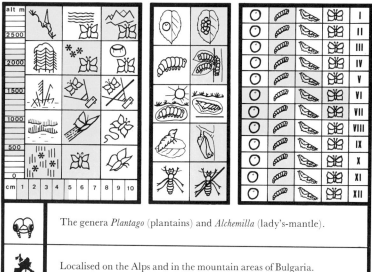

Euphydryas cynthia Schiffermüller ♂   Nymphalidae

The genera *Plantago* (plantains) and *Alchemilla* (lady's-mantle).

Localised on the Alps and in the mountain areas of Bulgaria.

Euphydryas aurinia Rottemburg ♀   Nymphalidae

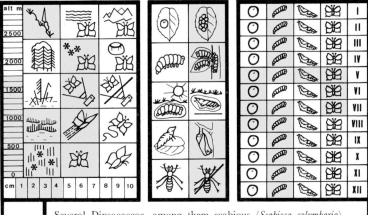

 Several Dipsacaceae, among them scabious (*Scabiosa columbaria*), *Succisa pratensis* and Plantains (*Plantago*).

 Northern Africa, western Europe, Russia, Asia Minor, temperate Asia as far as Japan.

Hipparchia semele L. ♂   Satyridae

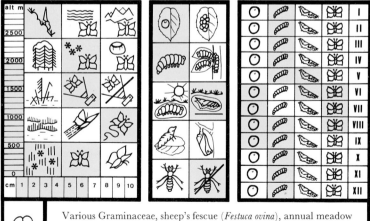

 Various Graminaceae, sheep's fescue (*Festuca ovina*), annual meadow grasses (*Poa annua*), false brome (*Brachypodium pinnatum*) and *Triticum*.

 Western Europe, central Europe to Russia and to the south of Armenia.

Arethusana arethusa Schiffermüller ♂   Satyridae

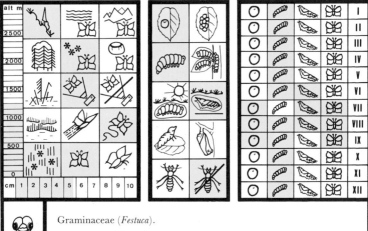

	Graminaceae (*Festuca*).
	Northern Africa, western Europe to central Asia.

Pyronia tithonus L. ♂ and ♀   Satyridae

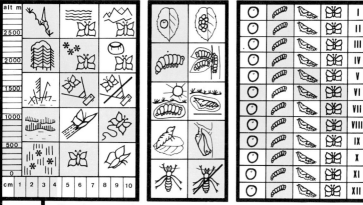

Graminaceae such as annual meadow grass (*Poa annua*), millet grass (*Milium*), false bromes (*Brachypodium*) and some Rosaceae of the genus *Rubus* (brambles).

Morocco, western Europe, Asia Minor, Caucasus.

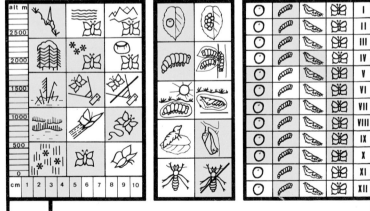

Maniola jurtina L. ♀   Satyridae

 Meadow grasses (*Poa annua*; *Poa pratensis*) and other Graminaceae.

Canary Islands, northern Africa, Europe to the Urals, Asia Minor and Iran.

Hyponephele lycaon Kuehn ♂   Satyridae

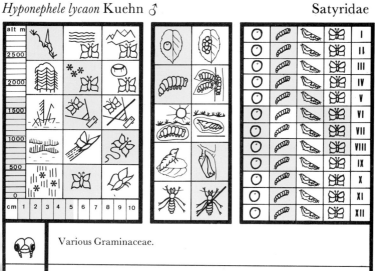

Various Graminaceae.

From western Europe to southern Russia; from Lebanon to the Caucasus and central Asia.

Coenonympha pamphilus L. ♂　　　　　　　　　Satyridae

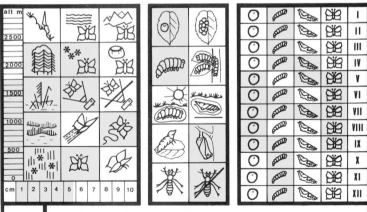

Various Graminaceae, mainly the genera *Poa* (meadow grasses, matgrass) and *Brachypodium* (false bromes).

From Europe to northern Africa and Asia Minor; Lebanon, Iraq and Turkestan to the east.

Coenonympha glycerion Borkhausen ♂   Satyridae

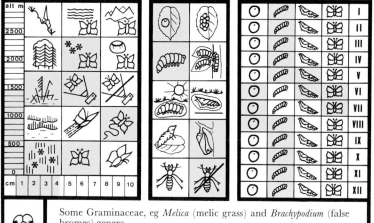

  Some Graminaceae, eg *Melica* (melic grass) and *Brachypodium* (false bromes) genera.

Western Europe and Russia as far as Siberia.

Coenonympha arcania L. ♀   Satyridae

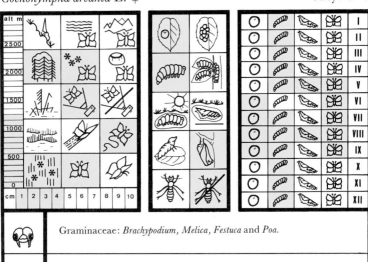

Graminaceae: *Brachypodium, Melica, Festuca* and *Poa.*

Western Europe to Asia Minor; southern Russia to the Urals.

Coenonympha dorus Esper ♂   Satyridae

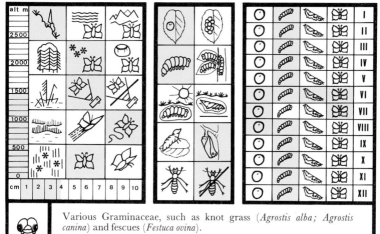

Various Graminaceae, such as knot grass (*Agrostis alba; Agrostis canina*) and fescues (*Festuca ovina*).

Southern Europe and northern Africa.

Pararge aegeria L. ♀   Satyridae

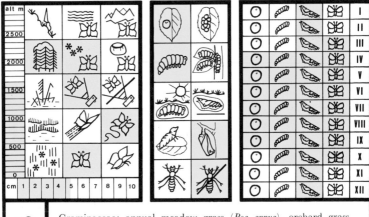

 Graminaceae: annual meadow grass (*Poa annua*), orchard grass (*Dactylis glomerata*) and chalk false brome (*Brachypodium pinnatum*).

Western Europe to Asia Minor and Syria, and as far as Russia and central Asia.

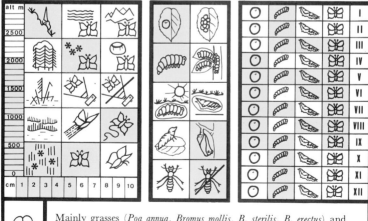

Lasiommata megera L. ♀   Satyridae

 Mainly grasses (*Poa annua, Bromus mollis, B. sterilis, B. erectus*) and sheep's fescue (*Festuca ovina*).

Western Europe, northern Africa, Russia, Asia Minor to Iran.

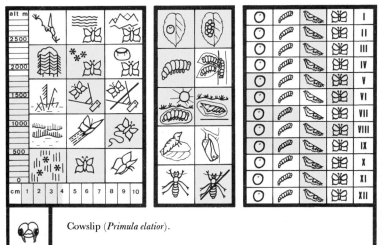

Hamearis lucina L. ♂

Nemeobiidae

Cowslip (*Primula elatior*).

From Europe to central Russia.

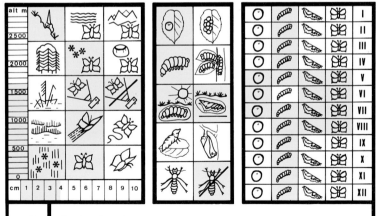

Thymelicus lineola Ochsenheimer ♂   Hesperiidae

 Various Graminaceae.

 Algeria and Morocco, western Europe, central Asia and North America.

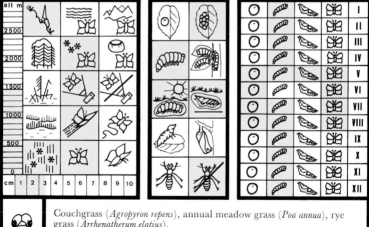

Thymelicus acteon Rottemburg ♀   Hesperiidae

Couchgrass (*Agropyron repens*), annual meadow grass (*Poa annua*), rye grass (*Arrhenatherum elatius*).

Europe to Asia Minor; Canary Islands.

Carterocephalus palaemon Pallas ♂ and ♀   Hesperiidae

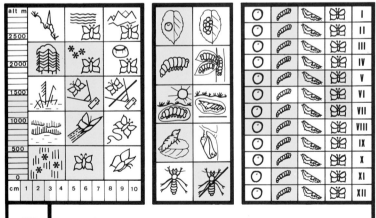

 Plantains (*Plantago lanceolata*) and couchgrass (*Agropyron repens*).

 Western Europe and Asia as far as Japan; North America.

Thymelicus sylvestris Poda ♂   Hesperiidae

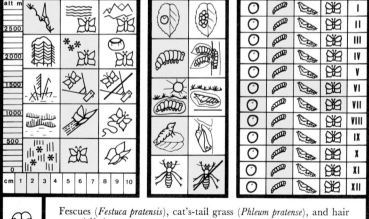

 Fescues (*Festuca pratensis*), cat's-tail grass (*Phleum pratense*), and hair grass (*Aira*).

Morocco, Europe to Asia Minor and Iran.

Hesperia comma L. ♀   Hesperiidae

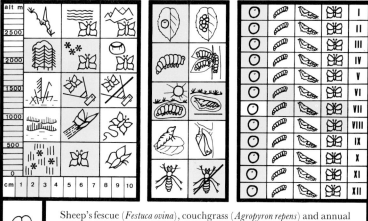

 Sheep's fescue (*Festuca ovina*), couchgrass (*Agropyron repens*) and annual meadow grass (*Poa annua*).

Northern Africa, Europe to temperate Asia; north-west of the United States.

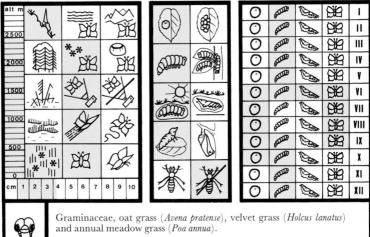

Ochlodes venatus faunus Turati ♀   Hesperiidae

Graminaceae, oat grass (*Avena pratense*), velvet grass (*Holcus lanatus*) and annual meadow grass (*Poa annua*).

Western Europe to temperate Asia as far as China and Japan.

Limenitis populi L. ♂   Nymphalidae

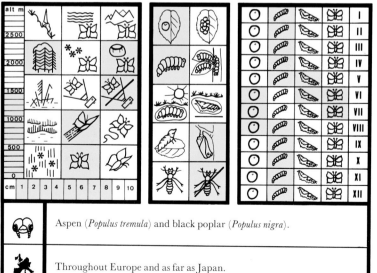

Aspen (*Populus tremula*) and black poplar (*Populus nigra*).

Throughout Europe and as far as Japan.

Limenitis camilla L. ♂

Nymphalidae

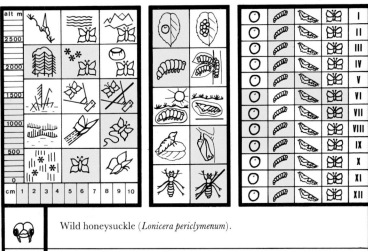

Wild honeysuckle (*Lonicera periclymenum*).

From western and central Europe to Russia, China and Japan.

Limenitis reducta Staudinger ♀　　　　　　　　Nymphalidae

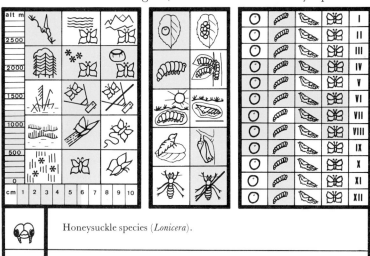

Honeysuckle species (*Lonicera*).

Southern and central Europe, western Asia, Syria, Caucasus, Iran.

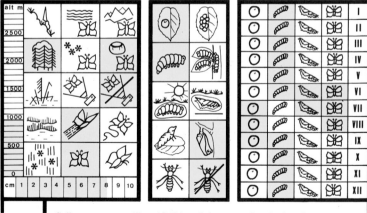

Apatura iris L. ♂   Nymphalidae

⊙	🐛	🦋	🦋	I
⊙	🐛	🦋	🦋	II
⊙	🐛	🦋	🦋	III
⊙	🐛	🦋	🦋	IV
⊙	🐛	🦋	🦋	V
⊙	🐛	🦋	🦋	VI
⊙	🐛	🦋	🦋	VII
⊙	🐛	🦋	🦋	VIII
⊙	🐛	🦋	🦋	IX
⊙	🐛	🦋	🦋	X
⊙	🐛	🦋	🦋	XI
⊙	🐛	🦋	🦋	XII

Sallow or pussy willow (*Salix*) and the genus *Populus* (poplar, aspen, etc).

Europe; temperate Asia as far as Japan.

Apatura ilia and *A. ilia f. clytie* Schiffermüller ♂   Nymphalidae

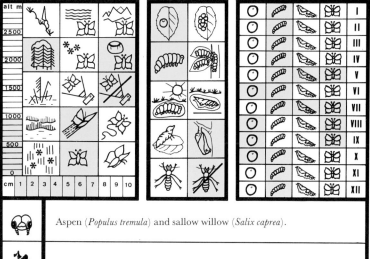

Aspen (*Populus tremula*) and sallow willow (*Salix caprea*).

Central and southern Europe; temperate Asia as far as Japan.

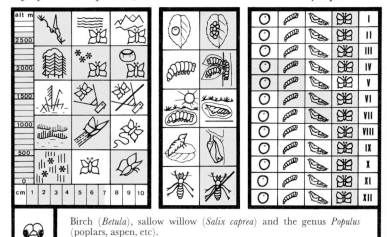

Nymphalis antiopa L. ♂   Nymphalidae

Birch (*Betula*), sallow willow (*Salix caprea*) and the genus *Populus* (poplars, aspen, etc).

From western Europe to temperate Asia, North America; now very rare in the UK.

Vanessa atalanta L. ♀   Nymphalidae

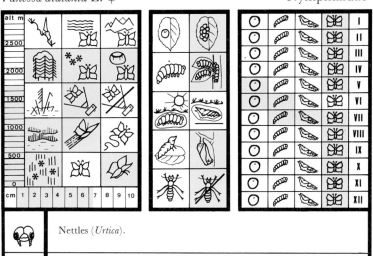

 Nettles (*Urtica*).

Azores, Canary Islands, northern Africa, Europe and Asia Minor; from North America to Guatemala; Haiti, New Zealand.

Hipparchia fagi Scopoli ♂   Satyridae

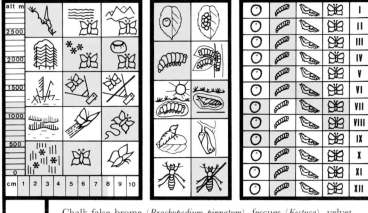

Chalk false brome (*Brachypodium pinnatum*), fescues (*Festuca*), velvet grass (*Holcus lanatus*) and feather grass (*Holcus mollis*).

From northern Spain to France and central Europe as far as the Balkans and southern Russia.

Hipparchia alcyone Schiffermüller ♂   Satyridae

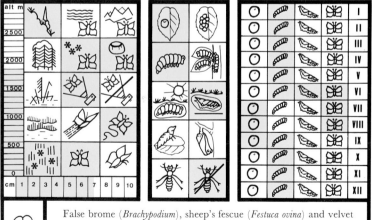

 False brome (*Brachypodium*), sheep's fescue (*Festuca ovina*) and velvet grass (*Holcus lanatus*).

 Northern Africa, central and southern Europe, Asia Minor.

Hipparchia statilinus Hufnagel ♂   Satyridae

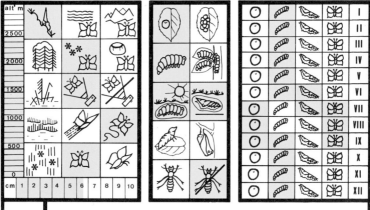

Annual meadow grass (*Poa annua*), brome grasses (*Bromus secalinus*), sheep's fescue (*Festuca ovina*) and hair grass (*Aira*).

Northern Africa, Iberian Peninsula, central and southern Europe to Asia Minor.

Chazara briseis L. ♂   Satyridae

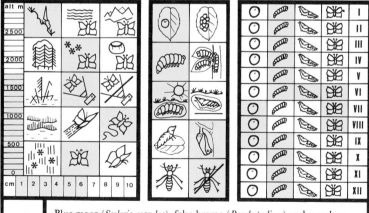

Blue moor (*Sesleria coerulea*), false brome (*Brachypodium*) and meadow grasses (*Poa*).

Northern Africa, mainly southern Europe as far as Asia (Iran, the Altai mountains and Pamir).

Brintesia circe Fabricius ♂   Satyridae

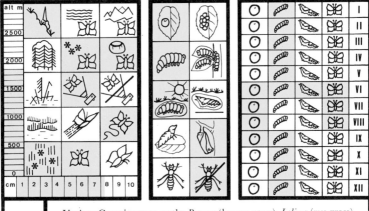

 Various Graminaceae, eg the *Bromus* (brome grass), *Lolium* (rye grass) and *Brachypodium* (false brome) genera.

Western Europe to Asia Minor and as far as Iran and the Himalayas.

Oeneis glacialis Moll ♂   Satyridae

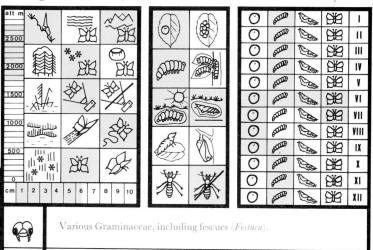

| | Various Graminaceae, including fescues (*Festuca*). |
| | Exclusive to the Alps. |

Satyrus actaea Esper ♂   Satyridae

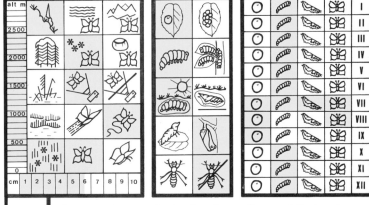

 Grasses of the genera *Brachypodium*, *Bromus*, *Festuca* and *Poa* (meadow grasses).

From south-west Europe to Asia Minor, Syria and Iran.

Satyrus ferula Fabricius ♂ 　　　　　　　　　　Satyridae

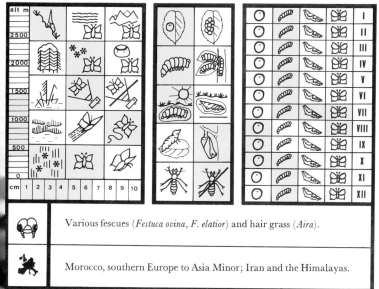

Various fescues (*Festuca ovina, F. elatior*) and hair grass (*Aira*).

Morocco, southern Europe to Asia Minor; Iran and the Himalayas.

Minois dryas Scopoli ♂   Satyridae

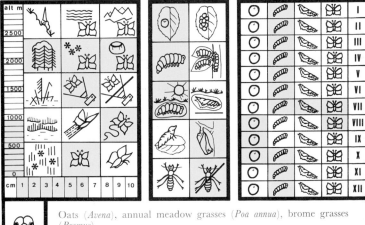

Oats (*Avena*), annual meadow grasses (*Poa annua*), brome grasses (*Bromus*).

Northern Spain to central Europe and central Asia as far as Japan.

Erebia aethiops Esper ♂   Satyridae

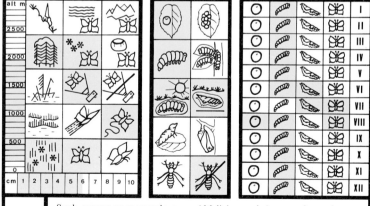

  Such grasses as mountain grass (*Molinia coerulea*), annual meadow grass (*Poa annua*), bent grass (*Agrostis canina*), orchard grass (*Dactylis glomerata*).

  Western Europe to Asia Minor, the Urals, the Caucasus and Sajan mountains.

Erebia ligea L. ♂   Satyridae

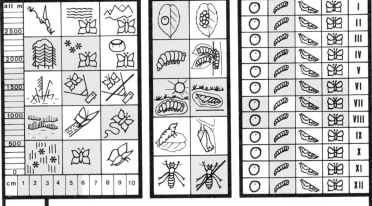

 Various Graminaceae, millet (*Milium effusum*), tufted hair grass (*Deschampsia caespitosa*), crabgrass (*Digitaria sanguinalis*).

Localised in Europe, the Kamchatka and Japan.

Erebia epiphron Knoch ♂   Satyridae

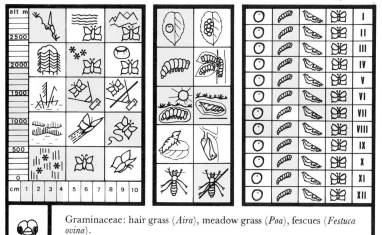

Graminaceae: hair grass (*Aira*), meadow grass (*Poa*), fescues (*Festuca ovina*).

European mountain regions.

Erebia medusa Denis and Schiffermüller ♀   Satyridae

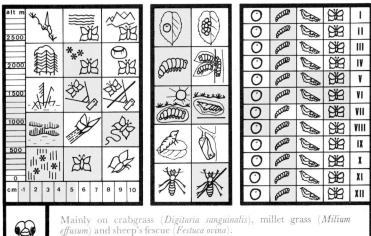

Mainly on crabgrass (*Digitaria sanguinalis*), millet grass (*Milium effusum*) and sheep's fescue (*Festuca ovina*).

From Europe to Asia Minor.

Lopinga achine Scopoli ♂   Satyridae

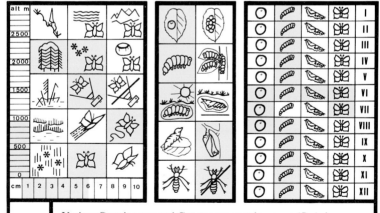

 Various Graminaceae and Cyperaceae, meadow grass (*Poa*), brome grass (*Bromus*) and rye grass (*Lolium*).

 Localised in the Pyrenees, throughout Europe as far as Russia, and central Asia to R. Amur; Japan.

Coenonympha hero L. ♂   Satyridae

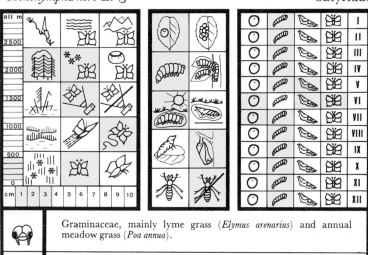

Graminaceae, mainly lyme grass (*Elymus arenarius*) and annual meadow grass (*Poa annua*).

Localised in western Europe, Scandinavia, central Europe to Asia, Korea and Japan.

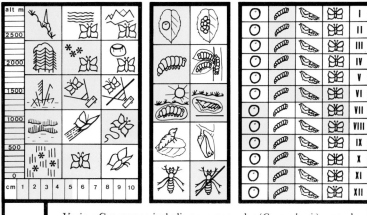

Aphantopus hyperantus L. ♂   Satyridae

 Various Cyperaceae, including common sedge (*Carex vulgaris*), several Graminaceae of the genus *Holcus* (eg velvet grass, feather grass).

Throughout Europe except for the south and the extreme north; Asia as far as R. Ussuri.

Thecla betulae L. ♂   Lycaenidae

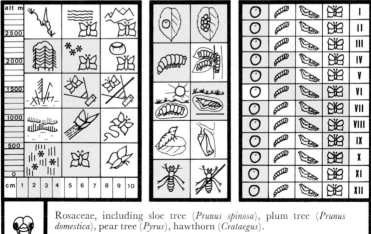

 Rosaceae, including sloe tree (*Prunus spinosa*), plum tree (*Prunus domestica*), pear tree (*Pyrus*), hawthorn (*Crataegus*).

From Europe to R. Amur and Korea.

Quercusia quercus L. ♀   Lycaenidae

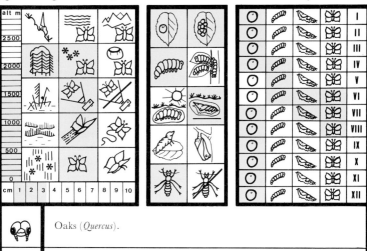

Oaks (*Quercus*).

Northern Africa, Europe; Asia Minor to Armenia.

Nordmannia ilicis Esper ♂   Lycaenidae

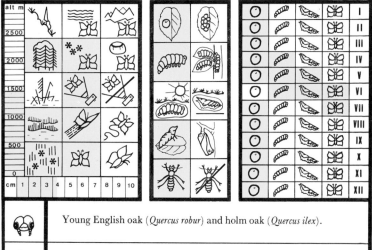

Young English oak (*Quercus robur*) and holm oak (*Quercus ilex*).

From Europe to Asia Minor.

Strymonidia spini Schiffermüller ♂   Lycaenidae

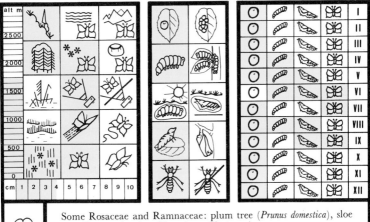

 Some Rosaceae and Ramnaceae: plum tree (*Prunus domestica*), sloe tree (*Prunus spinosa*) and hawthorn (*Crataegus*).

 From Europe to Asia Minor, Lebanon, Iraq and Iran.

Strymonidia w-album Knoch ♂   Lycaenidae

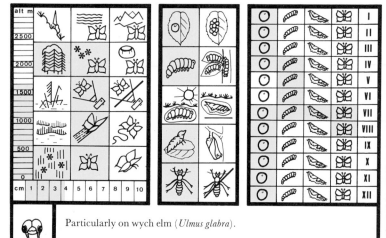

Particularly on wych elm (*Ulmus glabra*).

From Europe to Japan.

Lycaena helle Denis and Schiffermüller ♂   Lycaenidae

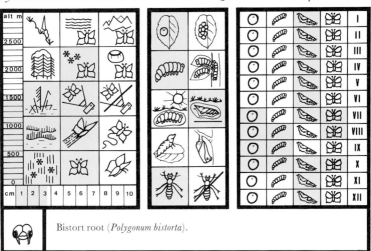

Bistort root (*Polygonum bistorta*).

From western Europe through Russia to Siberia.

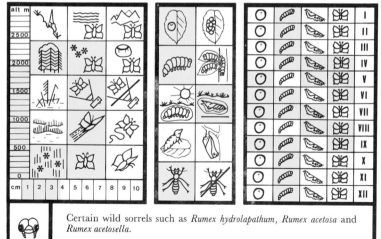

Heodes tityrus Poda ♂   Lycaenidae

Certain wild sorrels such as *Rumex hydrolapathum*, *Rumex acetosa* and *Rumex acetosella*.

From Europe through Russia to the Altai mountains.

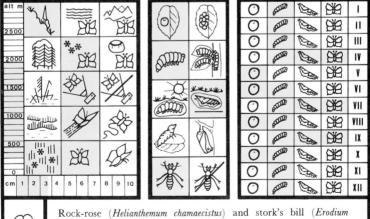

Aricia agestis Denis and Schiffermüller ♂   Lycaenidae

Rock-rose (*Helianthemum chamaecistus*) and stork's bill (*Erodium cicutarium*).

From Europe to R. Amur.

Pyrgus malvae L. ♂   Hesperiidae

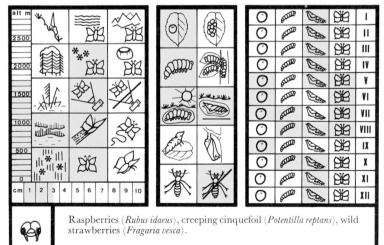

Raspberries (*Rubus idaeus*), creeping cinquefoil (*Potentilla reptans*), wild strawberries (*Fragaria vesca*).

From Europe to Mongolia as far as R. Amur.

Pyrgus alveus Huebner ♂ — Hesperiidae

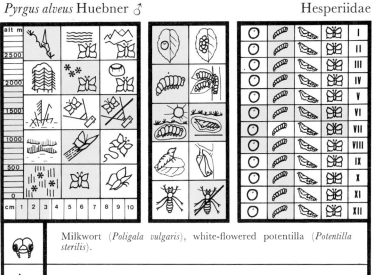

 Milkwort (*Poligala vulgaris*), white-flowered potentilla (*Potentilla sterilis*).

 Northern Africa, Europe, Caucasus, Altai mountains, Siberia.

Carcharodus alceae Esper ♂   Hesperiidae

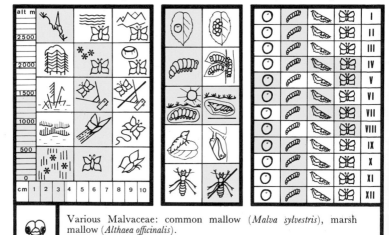

Various Malvaceae: common mallow (*Malva sylvestris*), marsh mallow (*Althaea officinalis*).

Northern Africa, southern and central Europe to Asia.

Spialia sertorius Hoffmannsegg ♂   Hesperiidae

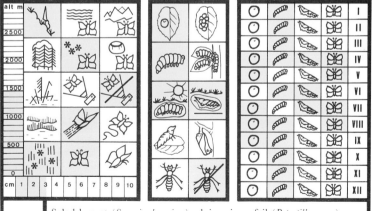

 Salad burnet (*Sanguisorba minor*), alpine cinquefoil (*Potentilla verna*), raspberry (*Rubus idaeus*).

 Northern Africa, southern Europe to western Asia, Altai mountains, R. Amur, Tibet.

Heteropterus morpheus Pallas ♂   Hesperiidae

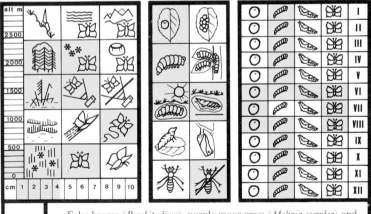

False brome (*Brachipodium*), purple moor grass (*Molinia coerulea*) and dog's-tooth grass (*Calamagrostis lanceolata*).

Localised in western Europe; more common towards the east, in central Asia and as far as Korea.

Erynnis tages L. ♂   Hesperiidae

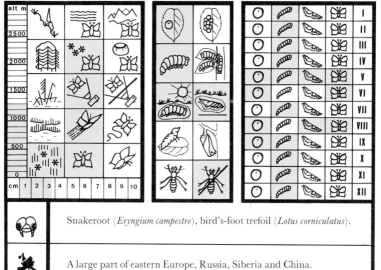

Snakeroot (*Eryngium campestre*), bird's-foot trefoil (*Lotus corniculatus*).

A large part of eastern Europe, Russia, Siberia and China.

Callophrys rubi L. ♂   Lycaenidae

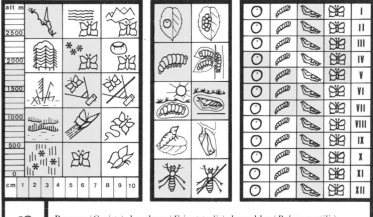

 Brooms (*Genista*), heathers (*Erica tetralix*), brambles (*Rubus saxatilis*).

Northern Africa, western Europe and as far east as R. Amur; Asia Minor; north-west of the United States.

Lampides boeticus L. ♀   Lycaenidae

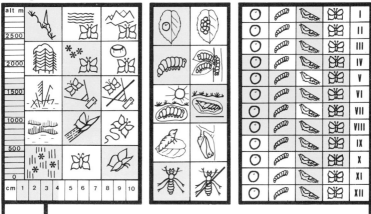

Bladder-nut tree (*Colutea arborescens*), lupins (*Lupinus*), furze (*Ulex*), sweet peas (*Lathirus*), clovers (*Trifolium*).

Africa, southern Europe; migrates to the north.

Tarucus rosaceus Austaut ♂   Lycaenidae

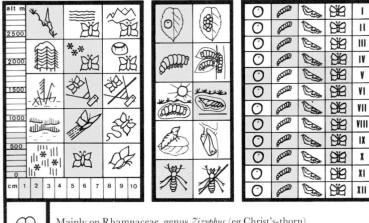

 Mainly on Rhamnaceae, genus *Zizyphus* (eg Christ's-thorn).

 Algeria, Tunisia, Arabia and western Asia, Iraq and Iran; above all in desert areas.

Syntarucus pirithous L. ♂   Lycaenidae

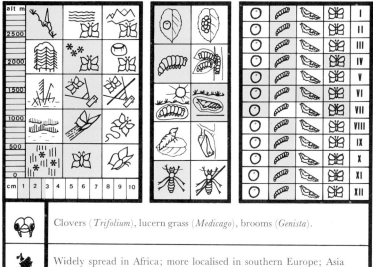

Clovers (*Trifolium*), lucern grass (*Medicago*), brooms (*Genista*).

Widely spread in Africa; more localised in southern Europe; Asia Minor.

Celastrina argiolus L. ♂   Lycaenidae

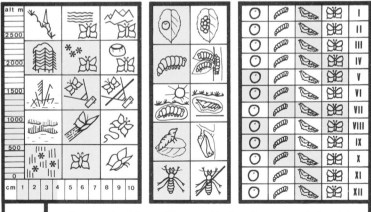

Common buckthorn (*Rhamnus cathartica*), flowers and fruits of the holly (*Ilex aquifolium*), flowers of the ivy (*Hedera helix*), ling (*Calluna vulgaris*).

From northern Africa to Europe and central Asia; Japan and the United States.

Glaucopsyche alexis Poda ♂   Lycaenidae

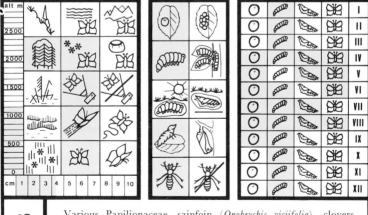

 Various Papilionaceae, sainfoin (*Onobrychis viciifolia*), clovers (*Trifolium*), lucern grass (*Medicago*), brooms (*Genista*).

From western Europe eastwards as far as Asia.

Maculinea alcon Denis and Schiffermüller ♂   Lycaenidae

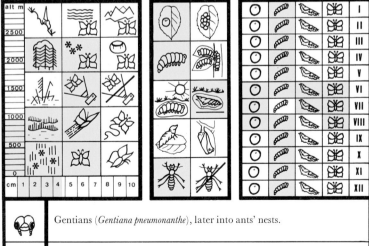

Gentians (*Gentiana pneumonanthe*), later into ants' nests.

Localised in Europe and as far as central Asia.

Maculinea arion L. ♂   Lycaenidae

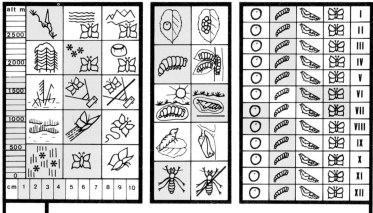

 Flowers of certain herbs: narrow-leafed thyme (*Thymus serpillum*), oregano (*Origanum vulgare*), later in ants' nests.

 From western Europe eastwards as far as China.

Plebejus argus L. ♂   Lycaenidae

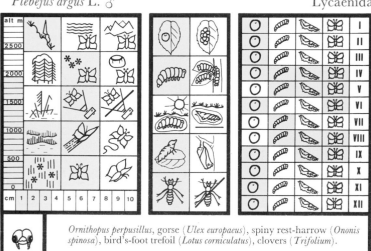

Ornithopus perpusillus, gorse (*Ulex europaeus*), spiny rest-harrow (*Ononis spinosa*), bird's-foot trefoil (*Lotus corniculatus*), clovers (*Trifolium*).

Europe to temperate Asia and Japan.

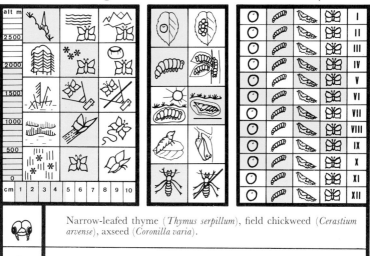

Philotes baton Bergstrasser ♂ and ♀   Lycaenidae

Narrow-leafed thyme (*Thymus serpillum*), field chickweed (*Cerastium arvense*), axseed (*Coronilla varia*).

Southern Europe as far as Asia Minor, Iran and Afghanistan.

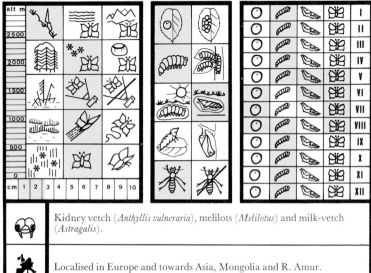

Cupido minimus Fuessly ♂   Lycaenidae

Kidney vetch (*Anthyllis vulneraria*), melilots (*Melilotus*) and milk-vetch (*Astragalis*).

Localised in Europe and towards Asia, Mongolia and R. Amur.

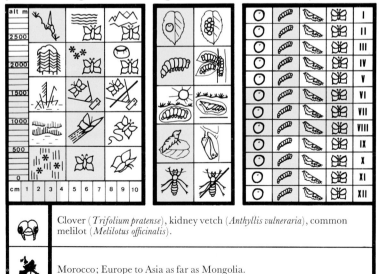

Cyaniris semiargus Rottemburg ♂   Lycaenidae

Clover (*Trifolium pratense*), kidney vetch (*Anthyllis vulneraria*), common melilot (*Melilotus officinalis*).

Morocco; Europe to Asia as far as Mongolia.

Agrodiaetus damon Schiffermüller ♂   Lycaenidae

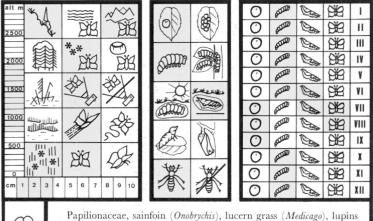

Papilionaceae, sainfoin (*Onobrychis*), lucern grass (*Medicago*), lupins (*Lupina*).

Mountainous areas of southern and central Europe as far as Armenia and the Altai mountains.

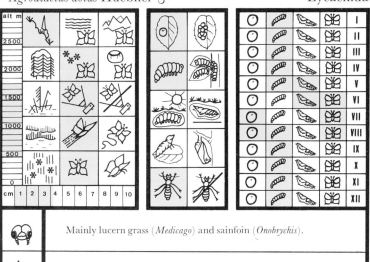

Agrodiaetus dolus Huebner ♂   Lycaenidae

Mainly lucern grass (*Medicago*) and sainfoin (*Onobrychis*).

Mountainous areas of northern Spain, Alps, Lozere mountains, Abruzzi.

Lysandra coridon Poda ♂ and ♀   Lycaenidae

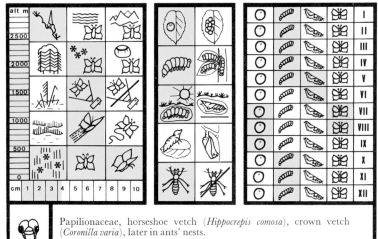

Papilionaceae, horseshoe vetch (*Hippocrepis comosa*), crown vetch (*Coronilla varia*), later in ants' nests.

Europe.

Lysandra bellargus Rottemburg ♂   Lycaenidae

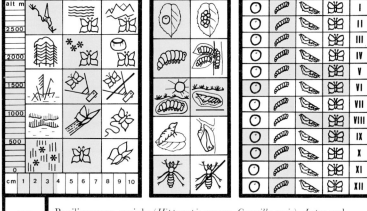

Papilionaceae, mainly (*Hippocrepis comosa, Coronilla varia*), *Lotus* and *Genista germanica*.

From Europe through Russia as far as Iraq and Iran.

Plebicula dorylas Denis and Schiffermüller ♂   Lycaenidae

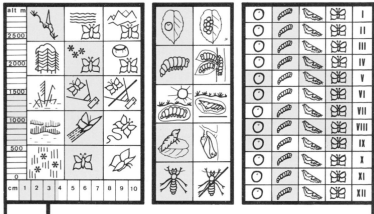

 Kidney vetch (*Anthyllis vulneraria*), narrow-leafed thyme (*Thymus serpillum*).

 From southern Europe to Asia Minor.

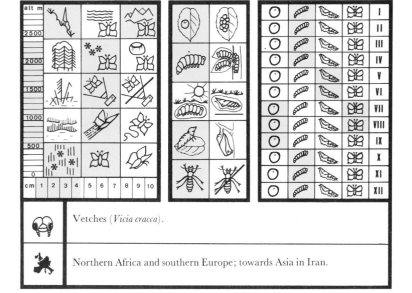

Plebicula amanda Schneider ♀   Lycaenidae

Vetches (*Vicia cracca*).

Northern Africa and southern Europe; towards Asia in Iran.

Meleageria daphnis Schiffermüller ♂   Lycaenidae

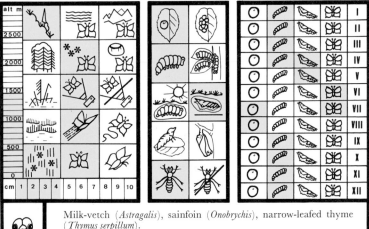

 Milk-vetch (*Astragalis*), sainfoin (*Onobrychis*), narrow-leafed thyme (*Thymus serpillum*).

Southern Europe and as far as Lebanon and Iran.

Iolana iolas Ochsenheimer ♂   Lycaenidae

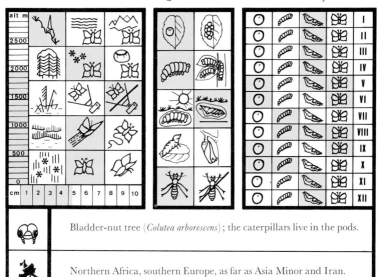

Bladder-nut tree (*Colutea arborescens*); the caterpillars live in the pods.

Northern Africa, southern Europe, as far as Asia Minor and Iran.

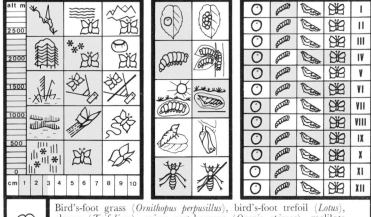

Polyommatus icarus Rottemburg ♂ and ♀   Lycaenidae

 Bird's-foot grass (*Ornithopus perpusillus*), bird's-foot trefoil (*Lotus*), clover (*Trifolium*), spiny rest-harrow (*Ononis spinosa*), melilots (*Mieilotus*).

 Canary Islands, northern Africa to the Sahara; Europe as far as Asia.

APPENDIX

Supplementary information related to:

1. Ecology (**E**): relationship between man and nature
2. Sexual dimorphism (**SD**): the differences between male (♂) and female (♀)
3. Certain variants (**V**): a description of a few peculiar forms

The figures correspond to those of the plates.

1. Swallowtail
E It is relatively rare to the north of its distribution area due to intensive cultivations of its favourite plant, the common carrot, which is treated with copper sulphates.
SD Very slight, ♀ is larger.
V *aurantiaca* S.: wing ground colour tinted with orange; *obscura* E.: wing ground black.

2. Corsican Swallowtail
E Like many other butterflies, this one is threatened by a scourge of our times, namely the woodland and scrubland fires which every year destroy thousands of acres thanks to the irresponsibility of a few picnickers. In Sardinia, the extensive eucalyptus plantations have also upset the ecological balance in many parts of the island.
SD ♀ is larger.
V *machaonides* V.: a hybrid of *P. machaon* and *P. hospiton*, very rare.

3. Southern Swallowtail
E Despite the highly localised hunting of caterpillars, this butterfly is still thriving in the Digne area in the Provençal Alps, where it is protected together with the rest of the flora and fauna.
SD ♀ larger and paler.
V *couleti* O.: the black band is much enlarged.

4. Scarce Swallowtail
E This marvellous species is protected in most parts of Europe.
SD ♀ larger.
V *zancleus* Z.: aestival brood, wing ground whitish; *nigrescens* E.: wing ground almost black.

5. Scarce Swallowtail (var.)
SD ♀ larger.

V *miegi* T.: vernal brood, displays a larger number of dark scales; *lotteri* A.: localised in northern Africa.

6. Southern Festoon
SD ♀ larger and with wider areas of red.
V *cassandra* H.: localised in the south of France and Italy, smaller and darker than the specimens of eastern Europe; *ochracea* S.: wing ground yellowish-ochre; *meta* M.: yellow patches on the hind-wings.

7. Spanish Festoon
SD ♀ larger.
V *africana* S.: localised in northern Africa, often with deeper colours; *honnorati* B.: extremely rare, red is the dominant colour on the wing ground; *hartmanni* S.: wing ground darker.

8. Apollo
E Splendid butterfly, often threatened, protected in many countries.
SD ♀ often darker, larger red ocelli. The body is smooth, the abdomen of fertilised females develops a sphragis (horny pouch).
V Extremely variable. The species includes innumerable distinct races, among them *nigracana* C.: wing ground is blackish.

9. Small Apollo
SD Unlike the previous species, the ♀ has a hairy, rather than smooth, abdomen. The red ocelli are larger.
V *gazeli* P.: localised in the Maritime Alps; *cardinalis* O.: the ocelli on the hind-wings are joined together.

10. Morocco Orange Tip
SD ♀ wing ground whitish.
V *euphenoides* S.: of southern Europe; the type species comes from northern Africa; *vernetensis* O.: the orange speck is not bordered with black.

11. Moorland Clouded Yellow
E The species is still well represented in the mountainous areas of northern Europe, in the Alps, the Jura and the Vosges mountains. It is very distressing to note how this beautiful species is disappearing from the Hautes-Fagnes region of Belgium, where the over-planting of spruces will soon completely deprive nature of one of its most beautiful specimens.
SD ♀ wing ground whitish.
V *europomene* on high summits; *philomene* D. (♀ form): wing ground yellowish rather than whitish.

12. Pale Clouded Yellow
SD ♀ whitish.
V ♀ *flava* H.: the ground colour of the wings is similar to the yellow of the ♂; *vernalis* V.: vernal brood, pale form.

13. **Berger's Clouded Yellow**
SD ♀ whitish, seldom yellowish; ♂ darker in colour than the preceding species.

14. **Brimstone**
SD ♂ saffron yellow, ♀ pale green.
V *meridionalis* R.: native of the Maghreb, very large and highly coloured; *britannica* O.: aberration ♀, wing ground yellowish; *cleodoxa* R.: no orange tip on the recto of the fore-wings.

15. **Cleopatra**
SD ♂ yellow and orange, ♀ wing ground cream, larger in size.
V *europaea* F.: native of southern Europe; the type species comes from Algeria.

16. **Marbled White**
SD ♀ larger, the dark patterns are duller.
V *lachesis* H.: from southern France and northern Spain; *lucasi* R.: from the Maghreb; *procida* H.: with smaller white parts; *leucomelas* E. (♀ form): the underside of the hind-wings has no patterns.

17. **Western Marbled White**
SD ♂ well-marked black patterns; ♀ larger patterns, duller.
V *peliaga* O.: native of Algeria and Morocco; *pherusia* B.: localised in Sicily (according to some scientists, this is probably a distinct species); *ixora* B.: absence of ocelli; *hubneri* O.: the underside of the hind-wings is rusty brown, the upper side of the fore-wings strongly darkened.

18. **Clouded Apollo**
SD ♀ larger, with a darker wing ground colour, smooth body ending with a clearly discernible sphragis.
V *herrichi* O.: form melanotic in the ♀; *helvetica* V.: alpine form; *pyrenaica* T.: pyrenean form; *alteres* M.: melanistic form.

19. **Black-veined White**
E The caterpillars of this species are considered to have a devastating effect on agriculture.
SD ♀ larger, fore-wings partly hyaline.
V *minor* O.: tiny, particularly in the mountains; *flava* T. (♀ form): the underside of the hind-wings is deep yellow; *melaina* T.: melanistic form.

20. **Large White**
E The caterpillar can damage the cultivation of Cruciferae.
SD ♂ white with a black margin on the fore-wings; ♀ larger, with black spots on the fore-wings.
V *chariclea* S.: vernal brood, quite large; *obscura* O.: becoming melanistic.

21. Small White
SD ♂ white, with a black margin on the fore-wings, ♀ larger, creamy with spots on the fore-wings.
V *metra* S.: vernal brood.

22. Green-veined White
SD ♀ has creamier wings with two spots on the fore-wings.
V *flavescens* V.: wing ground yellowish; *immaculata* F.: no black spots whatsoever on the fore-wings; *flava* K.: wing ground sulphur; *confluens* S.P.: the black spots are joined together; *bryoniae* H.: lives at high altitudes and the females are darker; *maura* V.: an Algerian form; *atlantis* O.: a Moroccan form.

23. Bath White
SD ♀ larger, with a greater number of black scales.
V *bellidice* O.: vernal brood, darker on the underside, paler on the upperside than the later broods; *anthracina* S.: form becoming melanistic.

24. Desert Orange Tip
SD ♀ has a greater number of black scales.

25. Orange Tip
SD ♀ without orange spots.
V *ochrea* T.: aberration ♀, the underside of the hind-wings is yellowish; *detersa* V.: aberration ♂ without orange spots, very rare; *lutea* G.: ♂ has yellowish rather than orange spots.

26. Dappled White
SD ♀ has clearer black patterns.
V *crameri* B.: mainly at medium and low altitudes; *insularis* S.: from Corsica and Sardinia.

27. Green-striped White
SD ♀ larger, sharper black patterns.

28. Mountain Clouded Yellow
SD ♀ whitish, ♂ yellowish.
V *oberthuri* V.: becoming melanistic.

29. Wood White
SD ♀ larger, the black spots are more blurred than the male's.
V *lathiry* H.: vernal brood, the underside of the hind-wings is touched with green; *erysini* B.: aberration ♂ completely devoid of spots; *subgrisea* S.: the underside of the hind-wings is grey; *sartha* H.: the underside of the hind-wings is yellow.

30. Clouded Yellow
SD ♀ with a greater number of black scales.
V *helice* H.: ♀ form, the ground colour of the wings is greyish to whitish

instead of orange; *obsoleta* T.: aberration ♀, the yellow patches have vanished from the upper border of the fore-wings.

31. Small Copper
SD ♀ the wings are rounder.
V *eleus* F.: aestival brood, larger and darker; *schmidti* G.: wing ground silvery white; *radiata* T.: the spots are linked, forming lines.

32. Large Copper
E The gradual drainage of marshlands in western Europe threatens this precious species, which is however protected in most countries.
SD ♀ displays a series of spots on the fore-wings.
V *aurata* L.: wing ground golden; *radiata* T.: the spots on the underside are linked to form lines. A second brood can appear in September only in exceptional years, but these specimens are less vividly coloured.

33. Scarce Copper
SD ♀ covered in dark scales.
V *montanus* M.: alpine form; *miegli* V.: local to the Iberian Peninsula; *elongata* C.: the spots on the underside are elongated into lines.

34. Purple-shot Copper
SD ♂ the wing ground is enhanced by a beautiful purple glaze; ♀ larger, without purple hues.
V *radiata* O.: the spots on the underside are linked to form lines; *gordius* S.: a form of southern Europe, the type species belongs to central Europe; *heracleanus* B.: a Moroccan form.

35. Lesser Fiery Copper
SD ♀ covered by a greater number of dark scales.
V *omphale* K.: aestival brood, displaying a small tail at the tip of the hind-wing.

36. Purple-edged Copper
SD ♀ with a greater number of dark scales.
V *eurydame* H.: belongs to the high summits of southern Europe, Alps, Pyrenees; *confluens* G.: the spots on the underside are lined; *stiberi* G.: form of the extreme north of Europe.

37. Plain Tiger
SD ♂ with androconial protrusions on the hind-wings; ♀ larger.
V *alcippus* F.: ♀ form with white hind-wings.

38. Nettle-tree Butterfly
SD ♀ larger and slightly duller.

39. Two-tailed Pasha
SD ♂ with vivid colours, ♀ larger and duller.
V *obsoleta* F.: the pale blue spots on the hind-wings have disappeared.

Important colonies of the Two-tailed Pasha still live in the Algerian oases; they probably represent a distinct subspecies.

40. Large Tortoiseshell
E In southern Europe the caterpillars of this species cause immense damage to fruit trees.
SD slight.
V *erythromelas* A.: from the Maghreb; *testudo* E.: melanotic. Aberrations are not rare.

41. Peacock Butterfly
SD slight.
V *balisaria* O.: the ocelli are blind; *ioides* O.: dwarf form.

42. Small Tortoiseshell
SD slight.
V *nigricaria* dM.: melanotic form; *pallida* T.: the ground of the wings is pinkish-white; *urticoides* FdW.: dwarf form; *ichnusa* H.: subspecies native of Corsica and Sardinia.

43. Painted Lady
SD slight.
V *pallida* S.: wing ground white, slightly tinged with pink; *melanosa* C.: melanotic form.

44. Comma Butterfly
SD ♀ wing margin more even.
V *hutchinsoni* R.: very large, tawny, pale yellowish, the wings are less indented; *variegata* T.: form with a vividly marbled underside, with green areas; *suffusa* F.: melanotic form of the type form; *album* E.: tending to melanism.

45. Map Butterfly
This is one of the rare species characterised by a strong seasonal dimorphism. Also typical is the way they lay their eggs, one on top of the other in hanging columns.
V *levana* L.: first (spring) brood, wing ground pale brown; *prorsa* L.: second brood, wing ground blackish; *porima* O.: wing ground blackish, the white parts are tawny.

46. Cardinal
SD ♀ larger.
V *lilicina* O.: rare, the underside of the hind-wings is violet rather than green; *paupercula* R.: with very few silvery marks on the underside; *violacea* T.: from northern Africa.

47. Silver-washed Fritillary
SD ♀ duller brown, larger black spots.
V *immaculata* B.: native to Corsica, Sardinia and Elba; *dives* O.: endemic to Algeria; *valesina* E.: ♀ form with the wings underside strongly tinted with green, sometimes violet; *anargyria* S.: lacks the

silvery bands on the underside of the hind-wings; *nigricana* C.: melanotic.

48. **Dark-green Fritillary**
SD ♀ larger and duller.
V *lyautey* O.: from Morocco, in the middle Atlas; *hortensia* R.: melanistic; *charlotta* H.: the silvery spots on the upperside of the wings are large and connected; *flavescens* T.: upperside of the wings tawny, pale yellowish.

49. **High-brown Fritillary**
SD ♀ larger.
V *chlorodippe* H-S.: from the Iberian Peninsula; *cleodoxa* O.: absence of nacreous spots on the underside; *thales* S.: melanotic; *isis* M.: the upperside of the wings is highlighted by pale ochre yellow.

50. **Niobe Fritillary**
SD ♀ larger and duller.
V *eris* M.: the nacreous spots on the upperside have been replaced by yellow spots; *obscura* S.: melanotic; *auresiana* F.: from Algeria and Morocco.

51. **Corsican Fritillary**
SD ♀ larger.

52. **Queen of Spain Fritillary**
SD ♀ larger and duller.
V *suffusa* T.: melanotic; *paradoxa* F.: irregular silver spots appear on the upperside of the hind-wings.

53. **Marbled Fritillary**
SD ♀ larger.
V a tendency to melanism is usual.

54. **Shepherd's Fritillary**
SD ♀ larger, the black patterns are wider.
V The type species can be seen in the eastern Alps; *palustris* F.: localised in the southern part of the French Alps up to the Brenner; *pyrenesmiscens* V.: from the Pyrenees to the Cantabrian mountains; *thales* S.: melanotic; *isis* M.: the upperside of the wings is highlighted with pale ochre yellow.

55. **Mountain Fritillary**
SD ♀s usually much darker.
V Aberrations are innumerable.

56. **Small Pearl-bordered Fritillary**
SD ♀ larger, with wider black patterns.
V Extremly variable, like the majority of the argynnis; *nigricans* O.: melanotic; *albinea* O.: albinotic.

57. Pearl-bordered Fritillary
SD ♀ larger.

V *albinea* L.: the ground colour of all four wings is a very pale ochre yellow, whitish, with typical black spots. There are innumerable aberrations, varying from the type form to forms with completely black wings; *pallida* S.: wing ground pale yellow; *obsoleta* T.: with no silvery spots.

58. Lesser Marbled Fritillary
SD ♀ larger.

V *lambini* L.: the upperside of the four wings is smokey brown, the underside of the fore-wings is marked by black spots; *tabusteani* O.: with a strong tendency to melanism.

59. Violet Fritillary
SD ♀ larger.

V *diniensis* O.: wing ground very bright, vivid tawny orange; *vittata* S.: the median band is wider and continuous.

60. Glanville Fritillary
SD ♀ larger.

V *atlantis* LC.: from the Moroccan High Atlas; *leucophana* C.: very light wing ground; *occitanica* S.: native of the Iberian Peninsula.

61. Knapweed Fritillary
SD ♀ very large.

V *punica* O.: from Algeria and Morocco. Forms tending to melanism are frequent.

62. Spotted Fritillary
SD ♀ larger and duller, wider black patterns.

V *meridionalis* S.: native to the mountains of central and southern Europe; *occidentalis* S.: native to southern Europe and northern Africa. An extremely variable species.

63. False Heath Fritillary
SD ♀ larger, not quite so black.

V *vernetensis* R.: from the Pyrenees, the Cantabrian and the Picos de Europa mountains; *corythalia* S.: albinotic form; *navarina* T.: melanotic form; *cordinai* S.: native of Spain, mainly Catalonia.

64. Heath Fritillary
SD ♀ larger and duller.

V *celadussa* F.: from southern Europe; *biedermanni* Q.: localised in Portugal and Spain; *navarina* dS.: strongly melanotic; *latonigena* S.: wing ground very light.

65. Nickerl's Fritillary
SD ○ duller.

V frequent tendency to melanism.

66. Scarce Fritillary
E This species is becoming increasingly rare and localised.
SD ♀ larger, the margin of the fore-wing is rounded.

67. Cynthia's Fritillary
SD ♀ larger, without white scales.

68. Marsh Fritillary
SD ♀ larger and duller.
V *provincialis* B.: from southern Europe; *beckeri* L.: widespread in Spain and Portugal, localised in France in the western Pyrenees, in Morocco in the Rif and middle Atlas; *barraguei* B.: Algerian form; *debilis* O.: limited to the high summits; *melanoleuca* C.: melanotic form.

69. Grayling
SD ♀ larger.
V *cadmus* F.: from central and southern Europe.

70. False Grayling
SD ♀ larger, bigger white spots.
V *suffusa* T.: ♂ aberration, without pale bands; *albina* O.: albinotic form.

71. Gatekeeper
SD ♀ larger and duller.
V Many races can be found in England.

72. Meadow Brown
SD ♀ larger, the wings spotted with orange.
V *hispulla* E.: southern form; *splendida* W.: localised in England and Ireland; *griseo-aurea* O.: albinotic form.

73. Dusky Meadow Brown
SD ♀ is characterised by two large black spots on the fore-wings.

74. Small Heath
SD ♀ larger.
V *lyllus* E.: from the Iberian Peninsula and northern Africa.

75. Chestnut Heath
SD ♀ characterised by more orangey fore-wings.

76. Pearly Heath
SD ♀ larger.
V *darwiniana* S.: form native to the Alps and Dolomites.

77. Dusky Heath
SD ♀ larger, with larger ocelli on the underside.

78. **Speckled Wood**
SD ♀ rounder fore-wings.
V *tircis* B.: native to northern and central Europe, the type species belonging to southern Europe and northern Africa; *intermedia* W.: an intermediate form between the type and *tircis*; *surnatior* dC.: melanotic form.

79. **Wall Brown**
SD ♀ larger and duller.
V *mediolugens* F.: albinotic form; *paramegaera* H.: native of Corsica and Sardinia.

80. **Duke of Burgundy Fritillary**
SD ♀ larger.
V *leucodes* C.: albinotic form. The second brood appears occasionally in the northern parts of its areas; it is darker in colour.

81. **Essex Skipper**
SD ♀ larger.

82. **Lulworth Skipper**
SD ♀ larger and darker.
V *oranus* E.: from the Maghreb.

83. **Chequered Skipper**
SD Slight.
V *nigra* D.: melanotic form.

84. **Small Skipper**
SD ♀ larger and lighter.
V *syriacus* T.: a large and beautiful race from southern Europe.

85. **Silver-spotted Skipper**
SD Slight.
V *suffusa* T.: a darker form.

86. **Large Skipper**
SD ♀ with some light spots on the fore-wings.

87. **Poplar Admiral**
SD ♀ very large, with wider white spots.
V *tremulae* E.: markings much darker.

88. **White Admiral**
SD ♀ larger, bigger white spots.

89. **Southern White Admiral**
SD ♀ larger, bigger white spots.
V *pythonissa* M.: absence of white-spotted band.

90. Purple Emperor
SD ♀ larger, without mauve reflections, fore-wings more rounded.
V At the beginning of the century, a large number of aberrations were recorded, among them: *iole* S.: entirely monocolour; *lugenda* C.: transition between *iole* and the type form.

91. Lesser Purple Emperor
SD ♀ larger, without mauve reflections, fore-wings more rounded.
V *iliades* M.: entirely monocolour; *leucothea* C.: aberration of the clytia form. The bands and spots of the four wings are white rather than yellowish; *astasicides* S.: aberration of the form clytia, brown without any pattern.

92. Camberwell Beauty
SD Slight.
V *hugiaea* H.: absence of blue spots and wider yellow band.

93. Red Admiral
SD Slight.
V *nana* S.: dwarf form; *millierei* C.: the typical red bands are replaced by white ones.

94. Woodland Grayling
SD ♀ larger, bigger white bands.

95. Rock Grayling
SD ♀ larger, wider white bands.

96. Tree Grayling
SD ♀ larger and duller.
V *sylvicola* A.: from the Maghreb; *albina* F.: albinotic form; *allonia* F.: an attractive race from Spain and Portugal.

97. The Hermit
SD ♀ larger, wider light areas.
V *pirata* E.: ♀ form, the whitish band which crosses the wings is tinted with ochre.

98. Great Banded Grayling
SD ♀ sometimes very large.

99. Alpine Grayling
SD ♀ larger and lighter.

100. Black Satyr
SD ♀ duller, with two ocelli on the fore-wings.

101. Great Sooty Satyr
SD ♀ larger, lighter ground colour, with two large tawny ocelli on the fore-wings.

102. Dryad
SD ♀ larger and lighter.

103. Scotch Argus
SD ♀ lighter ground colour.

104. Arran Brown
SD ♀ lighter ground.

105. Mountain Ringlet
SD Slight, ♀ duller.

106. Woodland Ringlet
SD ♀ lighter ground.

107. Woodland Brown
SD ♀ bigger ocelli.
V *anophtalma* O.: almost total absence of ocelli.

108. Scarce Heath
SD ♀ larger, orange ocelli are bigger.
V *areteoides* F.: absence of ocelli.

109. Ringlet
SD ♀ duller, larger ocelli.
V *arete* M.: much smaller ocelli.

110. Brown Hairstreak
SD ♀ larger, very beautiful, with a large orange band on the fore-wings.
V Extremely variable ♂; *jugurtha* O.: ground greyish brown; *unicolor* T.: ♂ without light patches on the fore-wings; *fisoni* W.: ♀ aberration, the orange band is ochre yellow.

111. Purple Hairstreak
SD ♀—the mauve reflections are limited to a spot on the fore-wing.
V *ibericus* S.: from the Iberian Peninsula to Morocco and Algeria; *obsoleta* T.: ♂ aberration without mauve reflections; *palescens* T.: the reflections are greyish green. Extremely numerous in certain years.

112. Ilex Hairstreak
SD ♀ with a large orange spot on the fore-wings.
V Extremely variable.

113. Blue-spot Hairstreak
SD ♀ larger.
V *lutea* T.: the spots are yellow rather than orange.

114. White-letter Hairstreak
SD ♀ larger.

V *butterowi* K.: there is no white line forming the characteristic letter 'W.'

115. Violet Copper
SD ♀ larger, without violet reflections.
V *obscura* M-R.: summer brood; darker on the upperside, lighter on the underside.

116. Sooty Copper
SD ♀ larger, the fore-wings are covered in orangey scales.
V *subalpinus* S.: dark form native to the Alps; *bleusei* O.: native of central Spain; *strandi* S.: the dots are elongated into lines; *circe* H.: melanotic form; *monterfilensis* O.: lighter ground.

117. Brown Argus
SD Slight.
V *radiata* O.: the dots are connected, forming lines.

118. Grizzled Skipper
SD Slight.
V *malvoides* E & E.: native to southern Europe, according to some this is a distinct species; *taras* B.: the white maculations on the fore-wings come together and form wide stripes.

119. Large Grizzled Skipper
SD ♀ larger.
V *centralitaliae* V.: native to central Italy; *alticolus* R.: from the Alps.

120. Mallow Skipper
SD ♀ larger.

121. Red Underwing Skipper
SD ♀ larger and duller.

122. Large Chequered Skipper
SD ♀ duller.

123. Dingy Skipper
SD ♀ lighter.
V *clarus* C.: greyish; *brunea* T.: brownish; *minor* L.: smaller.

124. Green Hairstreak
SD slight.
V *olivacea* B.: the underside is olive-greyish.

125. Long-tailed Blue
SD ♀ larger and browner.
V *ecaudata* O.: without tails; *grisescens* T.: a grey form.

126. **Mediterranean Tiger Blue**
SD ♀ larger and darker.

127. **Lang's Short-tailed Blue**
SD ♀ larger and browner.

128. **Holly Blue**
SD ♀ with a larger number of blackish scales.
V *parvipuncta* Fus.: summer brood, smaller.

129. **Green-underside Blue**
SD ♀ more tinted with black.

130. **Alcon Blue**
SD ♀ darker.
V *rebeli* H.: extremely localised as far as Denmark; *nigra* W.: melanotic; *cecinae* H.: without ocelli on the underside.

131. **Large Blue**
SD ♀ darker.
V *nigra* D.: melanotic; *obscura* C.: race native to the Alps; *ligurica* W.: from the French and Italian Riviera; *lycaonius* S.: total absence of ocelli on the upperside of the wings.

132. **Silver-studded Blue**
SD ♀ brown.
V *alpinus* H.: smaller form; *aegidion* M., from the Alps; *hypochionus* R., from the Iberian Peninsula; *corsicus* B.: from Corsica, Sardinia and Elba.

133. **Baton Blue**
SD ♀ brown, ♂ blue.

134. **Little Blue**
SD ♀ brown.

135. **Mazarine Blue**
SD ♀ brown.
V *striata* W.: the ocelli on the underside are joined into lines.

136. **Damon Blue**
SD ♀ brown.
V *agraphormena* V.: the white band on the underside of the hind-wings tends to disappear; *gillmeri* K.: without ocelli on the underside.

137. **Furry Blue**
SD ♀ brown, ♂ pale blue.

138. **Chalk-hill Blue**
SD ♀ brown.

V *syngrapha* K.: ♀ of the same colour as the ♂; *striata* T.: the ocelli are elongated into lines.

139. Adonis Blue
SD ♀ brown.
V *subtus-radiata* F.: the ocelli on the underside of the wings have changed into rays; *ceronus* E.: ♀ heavily sprinkled with blue spots.

140. Turquoise Blue
SD ♀ brown.
V *gabriellis* O.: in ♂ the upperside of the four wings is sprinkled with numerous, bright blue scales.

141. Amanda's Blue
SD ♀ brown, ♂ blue.

142. Meleager's Blue
SD ♀ darker.
V *steveni* T.: ♂ with a much darker wing upperside.

143. Iolas Blue
SD ♀ wing upperside sprinkled with brownish scales.

144. Common Blue
SD ♀ brown.
V *icarinus* S.: the black points on the underside of the wing's base are missing; *caerulescens* W.: ♀ form heavily sprinkled with blue.

GLOSSARY

Aberration: an individual variety of rare occurrence, a freak.

Albinism: total or partial absence of normal colour pigment.

Albinistic: affected by albinism.

Albinotic: tending towards albinistic.

Androconia: wing scales of special form, often tufted, occurring only in males and often in patches to form 'sex-brands'.

Biotope: habitat in which the main climatic, edaphic and biotic conditions are uniform.

Caudal: associated with the tail.

Cell (or discoidal cell): the area in the basal half of each wing generally enclosed by veins; when the closure is incomplete the cell is 'open'.

Cremaster: small hooked device used by a chrysalis to hang from its support.

Dimorphism: occurrence within a species of two distinct forms, or the differences between males and females of the same species.

Discal: of the disc or central area of the wing.

Discoidal: of the central area around the transverse discoidal veins at the end of the cell; discoidal spot is a conspicuous mark often present on those veins; discoidal cell is the central area enclosed by the veins.

Endemic: native to and always present in a particular area; often confined to that area.

Form: any recognisable distinct variant of a species (female form, seasonal form, local form, etc).

Hyaline: translucent, resembling glass.

Imago: the fourth phase of a butterfly's life, the adult insect (pl *imagines*).

Lunule: a crescent-shaped mark.

Melanism: colour variation due to excessive presence of melanin pigments making butterfly look very dark.

Melanotic: tending towards melanism.

Melanistic: affected by melanism.

Nacreous: like mother-of-pearl.

Ocellus: a round spot usually black with a central pale spot or 'pupil'; if the pupil is absent the ocellus is said to be blind.

Osmetecium: an organ situated on the back of a caterpillar's head and emitting a strong smell, off-putting to predators, at the slightest sign of danger.

Race: a local form with distinctive characteristics present in all or most individuals.

Sphragis: a horny, pouch-like structure formed underneath the female abdomen during copulation.

Subspecies: differing populations of a species occupying separate, although often contiguous, areas; geographical races.

Symbiosis: the association of the caterpillars of some butterflies with ants; literally, living together.

Type specimen: the specimen actually described by the author of the name of a species.

FURTHER READING

Brookes, M. and Knight, C., *A Complete Guide to British Butterflies*, J. Cape (1982)

Carter, D., *Butterflies and Moths*, Pan Books and The British Museum (1982)

Carter, D., *Observer's Book of Caterpillars*, Warne (1979)

Goodden, Robert, *British Butterflies: A Field Guide*, David & Charles (1978)

Higgins, L.G. and Riley, N.D., *A Field Guide to the Butterflies of Britain and Europe*, Collins (1980)

Parenti, U., *Butterflies and Moths*, Orbis Books (1972)

Parenti, U., *The World of Butterflies and Moths*, Orbis Publ (1978)

Wilkinson, J. and Tweedie, M., *Handguide to the Butterflies of Britain and Europe*, Collins (1980)

INDEX

WILD HERBS: A FIELD GUIDE
Jacques de Sloover and Martine Goossens

Whether used as a practical identification guide in the field, or for armchair browsing, this book offers a great deal of information succinctly presented. The herbs in the 144 stunning colour plates are grouped by colour. To identify a plant, simply open the guide at the pages bordered by the colour corresponding to that of the flower and you will soon find the plant itself. This ingenious system is time-saving, and the close proximity of illustrations of similarly coloured flowers helps to avoid misidentification.

For the purposes of this book, a herb is defined as a useful plant, one which is used to cure, to feed, to flavour dishes, to dye wool, or for any other specific aim. Pictograms presented alongside each colour plate summarise other properties – aromatic, medicinal and culinary, which parts are efficacious, when the herb is at its prime, where it grows, when it flowers. This at-a-glance information is supplemented by useful appendices, a glossary and notes on further reading.

210 × 120mm (8¼ × 4¾in) 144 colour illustrations, 144 pictograms

MUSHROOMS & TOADSTOOLS: A COLOUR FIELD GUIDE
U. Nonis

Anyone interested in collecting mushrooms, whether to study them scientifically or simply to enrich their everyday diet with their nutritional value, will find this book an invaluable guide. It is based on a new descriptive system: each of 168 colour photographs shows specimens in their natural habitat and is accompanied by a pictogram giving identification – at a glance – of their principal characteristics, combining a wealth of information with simplicity of presentation. Identification is further aided by the colours on the margins of the pages which reflect those of the fungi.

An introduction describes the main genera, their habitat, dangerous or valuable properties, and directions for collecting and growing them. Further Reading, Etymology of Scientific Terms and indexes contribute to the unique value of this guide.

210 × 120mm (8¼ × 4¾in) 168 colour illustrations, 79 line drawings, 168 pictograms

MINERALS & GEMSTONES: AN IDENTIFICATION GUIDE
Guiseppe Brocardo

A completely new way to approach the mineral world is here offered to the experienced collector and the beginner. The 156 splendid colour photographs are accompanied by a brief description and a pictographic table which provides, through easily recognisable symbols, the available information necessary for identification and classification. The key to the symbols is printed on a bookmark. The margins of the pages are coloured to reflect those of the minerals themselves and aid quick identification.

The colour plates are preceded by extensive information on how to recognise and collect minerals, their origin and formation, their structure and properties, the classification, and how to prepare them for preservation. A glossary, bibliography and indexes complete the volume and add to its value as an indispensable guide for all collectors.

210 × 120mm (8¼ × 4¾in) 156 colour illustrations, 27 line drawings, 156 pictograms

MOUNTAIN FLOWERS: A COLOUR FIELD GUIDE
S. Stefenelli

Thousands of enchanting flowers grow on the mountain slopes of Europe, and this book will prove an informative and useful guide for those wishing to discover more about them, while appreciating their beauty and understanding the need for their conservation.

Recognition is easy with the aid of the 168 splendid colour photographs. To identify a flower, simply match the colour of the flower to the corresponding colour section and your task becomes easy. Once it has been clearly identified, the pictograms which accompany the plates will enable the beginner and the serious botanist to discover at a glance all the other interesting facts about the flower. A bookmark showing the key to the pictogram, a section on habitat, a glossary of pharmaceutical terminology, a bibliography and two indexes add to the value of the book.

210 × 120mm (8¼ × 4¾in) 172 colour illustrations, 168 pictograms

FRESHWATER AQUARIUM FISH: A COLOUR GUIDE
J. P. Gosse

Fish, the most ancient vertebrates in the world, present an
amazing diversity of form, colour and mode of life. New
techniques for underwater exploration and means of transport
and storage have fostered an ever-increasing knowledge of their
ways and, with it, growing popularity for aquariums. Here you
will find the answers to most of the questions you are likely to
ask. Can the fish of your choice be placed in a tank where other
species already thrive? What sort of food will it need? How does
it reproduce? What temperature should the water be kept at? The
answers are condensed in the pictograms which accompany
each plate; these schematic little drawings, fully explained in the
text, allow you to see at a glance what temperament and
biological habit characterise your fish. The clarity of the 144
colour photographs is a precise guide to identification.

*210 × 120mm (8¼ × 4¾in) 144 colour illustrations, 144
pictograms*